SURVEY RESEARCH BY TELEPHONE

Volume 150, Sage Library of Social Research

RECENT VOLUMES IN
SAGE LIBRARY OF SOCIAL RESEARCH

105 Small **Was War Necessary?**
106 Sanders **Rape & Women's Identity**
107 Watkins **The Practice of Urban Economics**
108 Clubb/Flanigan/Zingale **Partisan Realignment**
109 Gittell **Limits to Citizen Participation**
110 Finsterbusch **Understanding Social Impacts**
111 Scanzoni/Szinovacz **Family Decision-Making**
112 Lidz/Walker **Heroin, Deviance and Morality**
113 Shupe/Bromley **The New Vigilantes**
114 Monahan **Predicting Violent Behavior**
115 Britan **Bureaucracy and Innovation**
116 Massarik/Kaback **Genetic Disease Control**
117 Levi **The Coming End of War**
118 Beardsley **Conflicting Ideologies in Political Economy**
119 LaRossa/LaRossa **Transition to Parenthood**
120 Alexandroff **The Logic of Diplomacy**
121 Tittle **Careers and Family**
122 Reardon **Persuasion**
123 Hindelang/Hirschi/Weis **Measuring Delinquency**
124 Skogan/Maxfield **Coping With Crime**
125 Weiner **Cultural Marxism and Political Sociology**
126 McPhail **Electronic Colonialism**
127 Holmes **The Policy Process in Communist States**
128 Froland/Pancoast/Chapman/Kimboko **Helping Networks and Human Services**
129 Pagelow **Woman-Battering**
130 Levine/Rubin/Wolohojian **The Politics of Retrenchment**
131 Saxe/Fine **Social Experiments**
132 Phillips/Votey **The Economics of Crime Control**
133 Zelnik/Kantner/Ford **Sex and Pregnancy in Adolescence**
134 Rist **Earning and Learning**
135 House **The Art of Public Policy Analysis**
136 Turk **Political Criminality**
137 Macarov **Worker Productivity**
138 Mizruchi **The American Corporate Network**
139 Druckman/Rozelle/Baxter **Nonverbal Communication**
140 Sommerville **The Rise and Fall of Childhood**
141 Quinney **Social Existence**
142 Toch/Grant **Reforming Human Services**
143 Scanzoni **Shaping Tomorrow's Family**
144 Babad/Birnbaum/Benne **The Social Self**
145 Rondinelli **Secondary Cities in Developing Countries**
146 Rothman/Teresa/Kay/Morningstar **Marketing Human Service Innovations**
147 Martin **Managing Without Managers**
148 Schwendinger/Schwendinger **Rape and Inequality**
149 Snow **Creating Media Culture**
150 Frey **Survey Research by Telephone**

SURVEY RESEARCH BY TELEPHONE

JAMES H. FREY

Volume 150
SAGE LIBRARY OF
SOCIAL RESEARCH

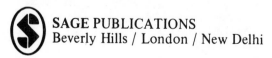

SAGE PUBLICATIONS
Beverly Hills / London / New Delhi

For information address:

SAGE Publications, Inc.
275 South Beverly Drive
Beverly Hills, California 90212

SAGE Publications India Pvt. Ltd.
C-236 Defence Colony
New Delhi 110 024, India

SAGE Publications Ltd
28 Banner Street
London EC1Y 8QE, England

Printed in the United States of America

Library of Congress Cataloging in Publication Data

Main entry under title:

Frey, James H.
    Survey research by telephone.

    (Sage library of social research ; v. 150)
    Includes bibliographical references and indexes.
    1. Telephone surveys.   2. Social sciences—
Research.   I. Title.   II. Series.
H91.F73   1983   001.4'33   83-3094
ISBN 0-8039-1996-4
ISBN 0-8039-1997-2 (pbk.)

THIRD PRINTING, 1985

CONTENTS

Preface   7

1. Introduction   9
2. Comparing Survey Methods   27
3. Sampling   57
4. Questionnaire Design   87
5. Administration   129
6. Final Considerations and the Future   171

Appendix A   189
Appendix B   193
References   195
Author Index   202
Subject Index   205
About the Author   208

PREFACE

This book was written for the person who has some familiarity with surveys in general and who desires additional information on how to implement one particular type of survey—the telephone survey. More than likely, this person will be someone like myself who directs a medium- or small-scale operation and who desires, at times, to utilize a telephone survey to meet a particular research need. The material contained in the chapters which follow includes a discussion of the place of the telephone in social and economic life; it will compare the telephone survey to mail and face-to-face survey techniques, and there is a description of the procedures necessary for drawing a sample, designating a questionnaire, and implementing an administrative plan for a telephone survey. Certainly one's research situation will call for adaptations of the procedures described, and not all of the information required to conduct a telephone survey will be contained in this treatise. Very often, conducting a survey is a matter of style, but following standardized procedures such as those suggested in this text will prevent an excessive compromise of data quality in the name of research artistry.

Throughout the text I have noted that the telephone survey has many advantages over other types (lower cost, less time for completion, and so forth). At no time do I want to imply, however, that the telephone survey is any "easier" to implement than the face-to-face or mail survey. On the contrary, I want to emphasize that conducting telephone surveys requires just as much attention to organizational and procedural matters as any other type of research. It is misleading to assume that a telephone survey can be "quick and dirty" at a lower price. If this is your conception of telephone survey research, it is incorrect. A thorough reading of this text should demonstrate that most telephone surveys are complex and demanding, not simple and easy.

At this time I would like to acknowledge several persons who assisted me in the preparation of this manuscript. Lillian Havis, Debra Duddleston, Judy Robinson, and Carol Frey provided typing assistance on earlier drafts. Joyce Standish supplied invaluable editorial input. Special thanks go to Jim Richardson, JoAnn Nigg, Morrie Axelrod, and a Sage reviewer who read all or part of earlier drafts. Finally, a great deal of the material in this book reflects the inspiration and tutelage of my friend and former advisor, Don A. Dillman. Even with this able assistance, errors remain, but they are of my own making.

—James H. Frey
University of Nevada, Las Vegas

CHAPTER 1

INTRODUCTION

In the history of survey research, no other technical or procedural innovation, with the exception of the computer, has made
as significant an impact on this type of data gathering as the
telephone. It is safe to say that within the last five years or so,
surveys by telephone have achieved some equity with the more
traditional face-to-face technique in terms of frequency of use
and methodological attention. A significant portion of this shift
can be attributed to the rising costs and declining response rates
experienced by the face-to-face survey. These factors have made
this technique less attractive to survey researchers, particularly
those working within severe constraints on time and money. On
the other hand, the rise to prominence of surveys by telephone
is also the result of improved telephone technology, improved
telephone research procedures, and the nearly complete accessibility of any population via the telephone. As a result of these
factors, many researchers who had habitually depended on the
face-to-face interview have had to reorganize their approach to
survey research and increase their use of telephone surveys. This
book describes the technical and methodological development
of telephone surveys, beginning with a brief history of the
telephone and its use. The text continues by outlining how this
type of data gathering can generate reliable information for
social scientists, policymakers, commercial research firms, and
others who would utilize survey research.

History of the Telephone

Throughout history there have been technological innovations that contributed greatly to the transformation of everyday

life. The radio, automobile, telegraph, television, electric light, and of course, the telephone, are some examples. Not only have these devices reduced problems related to time and distance, they have also had impacts on social relations and human behavior. Long neglected by social scientists, the telephone's impact on behavior may be more pronounced than any other technological innovation of the modern industrial era.

Few survey researchers have looked at the telephone from any other perspective than a technological one; that is, adapting hardware to survey needs. This is unfortunate, since it is possible that understanding the social significance of the telephone and how it conditions certain behavior patterns may provide some insights regarding certain patterns of response (for example, refusals) that survey researchers encounter. To fully comprehend this phenomenon, it is important first to outline the history and social significance of the telephone in American life.

When Alexander Graham Bell presented the telephone for patent in 1876, he was one of many who had been working on a process to transmit speech electronically. In fact, Bell's patent application was filed only one hour before that of Elisha Grey (McLuhan, 1964: 269). The first telephone was a successor to the telegraph, which had been invented some forty years before, and preceded by another forty years the invention of the radio by Marconi.

In its early history, the telephone was viewed as an "electrical toy" (Aronson, 1977); few people could see any use for it. At that time, the telegraph was the most prominent communicating device, as evidenced by an extensive network of telegraph stations and lines stretching across the country. In addition, the telegraph was preferred because it left a permanent record, while the telephone did not. Since two-way communication was not possible in early phone technology, the first telephones were marketed as a broadcasting or entertainment medium similar to the still-to-be-invented radio (Briggs, 1977). Concerts by a chorus of young ladies, news broadcasts to a central location, such as a tavern or general store, and recitations of Shakespeare to audiences gathered at fairs or expositions were representative of the first uses of the telephone.

As with most inventions, the prominent and well-to-do were the first to realize the utility of this device. In 1879, Lord Salisbury, British Prime Minister at the time, recited nursery rhymes to astonished guests from a "mysterious instrument on a neighbouring table" (Briggs, 1977: 41). Very often one of the 230 or so American subscribers who could afford its installation would invite guests to a party that would feature a musical concert, dramatic presentation, or lecture by means of the telephone. Even Alexander Graham Bell was known to entertain at these functions with lectures on electricity, and his compatriot, Thomas Watson, would sing the latest popular tunes. In fact, in the first telephone transmission to Boston from New York, Bell played "Yankee Doodle" on an organ and asked the receiving telegraph operator to "name that tune" (Aronson, 1977). These examples demonstrate that in its early years, the telephone was essentially a device of pleasure and novelty rather than an instrument for practical use in everyday affairs. This was soon to change, however, as "pleasure telephoning" gave way to routine conversational use.

The routinization of telephone usage began when two way communication became possible. In fact, Bell and Watson took only eight months after the original March 10 patent date to present a telephone device that could satisfactorily carry two-way conversations. Nevertheless, the inventors continued to market radiolike broadcasts to satisfy the interests and demands of their financial backers, who saw this as the best way to recoup their investment and to popularize the instrument. From its inception, Bell conceived of the telephone as a device to reduce the barriers of time and distance by allowing separated friends, family, and business associates to talk to each other directly. But it was not until the installation of a central exchange with the appropriate switching mechanism that the telephone began to move from its novelty status to one of practicality.

The first experimental telephone exchange was established in Boston in 1877 and, interestingly enough, the first switching stations were located in commercial banks. The exchange concept became popular only when business interests saw the potential in the telephone for organizing their daily affairs, for information gathering, and for expanding their markets. This was a time when corporate powers needed to raise money quickly, and the phone was simple to operate and left no written record. This fact was not lost on the "Robber Barons," since messages of the times often carried violations of the anti-trust laws (Aronson, 1977). The hotel industry was also one of the first to see the potential of the phone, since it provided a mechanism whereby executives could operate out of the hotel and still keep in touch with their businesses. Thus, the early history of telephone usage is one of business and commercial domination, with residential areas represented by only 11 percent of the total subscribers and limited to the well-to-do who could afford the $100-200 monthly fees.

The only way the average citizen could use the telephone in its early history was to go to a bank or drugstore to use a "pay phone" for five cents. The caller could make contact with a friend or business establishment. At the same time, one could catch up on the latest local gossip by quizzing the telephone operator at the central switchboard. It did not take long, however, for the dispersion of the telephone to reach unprecedented dimensions, even in the early decades of the century. Several factors contributed to this phenomenon. First, people recognized that the phone was much easier to use than the telegraph. It was not necessary to learn a special communicating code, nor did one have to wait for a reply message. Second, after Bell's patent expired in the 1800s, competition developed with Bell's company, American Telephone and Telegraph. The presence of other telephone companies in the marketplace pushed down prices and increased the telephone's dispersion. By the end of World War II, the telephone was available to even the poorest segments of the population. Third, America's industrial sector found that it could decentralize its operations, locating factories in cities and states at some distance from the central office, because of developments in transportation and because of concomitant improvements in long distance, two-way telephone communication.

Today, the United States leads the world in the absolute number of phones and is second only to the principality of Monaco in the number of phones per 100 inhabitants (United Nations, 1981). Virtually every American household has a phone. The latest figures for the United States show that there are 730 phones per 1000 population, 130 million residential phones in use, 1082 million conversations daily, and telephones in 98 percent of American households. In fact, nineteen states have 100 percent phone coverage, and twenty states can claim 95-99 percent coverage (U.S. Bureau of the Census, 1981). No other device, except perhaps television, can claim such ubiquity. The telephone is an omnipresent technological appendage of American life. Its significance, however, rests not with its mere technological presence, but with the social and behavioral changes that have come about as a result of the telephone's full-fledged adoption by the American public.

Impact on Social Relations

Arthur Pound (1926), in his book, *The Telephone Idea: Fifty Years Later,* asserted that the telephone was actually three things: (1) a cohesive force for the nation, (2) an antidote for sectionalism, and (3) an invigorator of trade. Both Pound and Alexander Graham Bell recognized that the telephone had the potential to make significant organizational, economic, and social impacts on society.

New forms of social organization became possible that no longer required persons to be located at fixed points (Perry, 1977). Thus the telephone was a great device of personal and geographical emancipation. Economically, the telephone reduced what Aronson (1971) calls "transaction time" for doing business, and it made industrial decentralization possible by enabling companies to locate various parts of their operations at some distance from each other. The stock, bond, and commodity markets were able to expand beyond Wall Street, thus enabling production to be separate from marketing or administration. Time and distance were no longer obstacles to business dealings, nor to the supervision and control of satellite enterprises. Even shopping patterns were changed with the introduction of the ultimate buyer's guide—The Yellow Pages.

The telephone also had a significant impact on social relations. The nature of modern urban life, particularly the separation of workplace and residence, and the development of modern suburbia can be attributed to a large extent to the development of the telephone. The telephone made it possible for personal relations and multilevel commitments to be established and maintained beyond the immediate living area. An extended family could be kept together even as members of that social unit were scattered to various regions of the country. New concepts of the "psychological neighborhood," "conceptual environment," or "symbolic proximity" referred to the ability of persons no longer living in contiguous housing units or sharing group experiences to maintain a social bond as the result of being in contact by telephone.

The telephone became a mechanism that helped to reduce the effects of isolation, alienation, fear, and insecurity which resulted from a relocation to unfamiliar surroundings. It permitted the retention of the old community network (Keller, 1977), which became a source of protection, therapy, and sociability. Thus, if the phone promoted the decomposition of neighborhoods, it was also instrumental in retaining membership in old neighborhoods while easing the transition into new ones. In fact, it is still true today that the households that are the highest users (based on number of outgoing calls) are those containing families that have just moved into a new neighborhood (Meyer, 1977).

The telephone is also a mechanism for relief from boredom. Very often the phone provides one's only access to the outside world. Jack Paar tells the story of a woman who called him and said that she was so lonesome that she took a bath three times a day in hopes that the phone would ring (McLuhan, 1964: 265). The desire to reduce the effects of isolation explains, to some degree, the behavior of the eager respondent who will talk for what seem to be hours in response to the simplest of questions, or who seems to be utilizing the interview for therapeutic reinforcement rather than a simple information-sharing device. For many, the possession of a telephone is a mitigating factor in reducing the harsh effects of a continually changing urban lifestyle.

Human Behavior and Telephone Usage

The telephone is a technological innovation that has altered our social relations perhaps more than any other device, including the automobile (McLuhan, 1964). It has become an extension of ourselves. It is even more of an embodiment of ourselves than the other media, because its requirements for our attention and concentration are much greater; the telephone demands our complete participation, whereas the other media do not. We read the paper while drinking coffee or eating breakfast. We can play cards, read a magazine, eat dinner, or converse with friends while watching television. And almost any other activity can accompany listening to the radio. However, when on the telephone, and particularly when engaged in an instrumental activity (for example, answering poll questions), complete attention is required. Many may not be ready to give their undivided attention to a telephone conversation because they are used to sharing their attention to any media event with other demands. In fact, it is possible that reluctance to be totally consumed by a telephone interview request could explain why some persons refuse to be interviewed or answer in an evasive or incomplete fashion.

Engaging in conversation via the telephone can also produce a great deal of anxiety on the part of respondents because there are no visual cues that one can utilize to predict the status or social categories of the caller. There is immediate equality but also a great deal of uncertainty in each phone contact, particularly in the early stages of the call (McLuhan, 1964). Usually we want to compare our social position to that of another in order to inject certainty and predictability into social relations. If we cannot do this, we are uncomfortable in that social context, and we may want to relieve that uneasiness by a quick termination of the relationship. This is why an introductory statement is so crucial to obtaining a complete interview; its first task is to relieve any potential anxiety by providing the respondent with full information about the source and nature of the call.

NORMS OF TELEPHONE USAGE

There are several norms of behavior surrounding phone usage. First, the ringing phone creates tension to the point that we feel a compulsion to answer the ring. Some of us even feel the urge to answer a ringing public telephone when we know that the call cannot be for us. The phone is a participant in life; it demands a partner. The ring calls for completion or closure (McLuhan, 1964). The phone is not a background instrument but a dominant participatory feature in any setting in which it is included, and its ring calls loudly for response.

It is as if we have been conditioned to respond; not to answer would mean risking the loss of a potentially rewarding social interaction or message (Ball, 1968). Hence, it takes a significant diversion not to answer the phone. For a telephone researcher, this means that if the phone rings in the home of a potential respondent, it will probably be answered. The compulsion to answer guarantees some success for phone solicitors and has contributed significantly to the proliferation of telephone sales promotions (and telephone surveys, I might add).

Second, the survey researcher can take advantage of another norm of telephone behavior which holds that it is the "initiator of the call who shall terminate that call" (Ball, 1968). Hanging up is very difficult, since it would represent what Ball has called "interactional homicide." Hanging up has the irrevocable effect of killing the dyad. Few of us are able to just "hang up"; rather, we somehow negotiate our intention not to participate. The fact that there are few flat-out hang-ups in telephone work may be the result of the pressure of this norm. Skillful interviewing (that is, the ability to negotiate access to a respondent who is inclined not to participate) is important. Surveyors can take advantage of the fact that respondents are not likely to thwart their appeal by a deliberate cutoff.

A third norm of telephone behavior is that interactional obligations require active participation in the conversation. Thus, whatever the question, respondents will provide an answer, even if it is a rather undefinable "grunt." This signifies continued attention and also satisfies the interviewer's need to obtain a response to a question. Silence is a rare occurrence in most phone conversations.

A telephone conversation is an interactional sequence without the assistance of visual cues. Each call begins in a situation of equality and evolves into differences. Thus, any telephone conversation is a strategy for the instrumental presentation of self and the control of others "through image vending so as to evoke the desired response" (Ball, 1968). Nonvisual cues are assumed to be actual representations of self and, if done skillfully, trust is established. These conditions seemingly give the survey researcher an advantage in the calling situation. When a call is made, each respondent feels an obligation to answer, an obligation to negotiate termination, and a pressure to carry on an active part in the conversation. All this is accompanied by an initial feeling of trust that the call is motivated by a legitimate desire for help from the respondent. Erosion of that trust can occur in the first few seconds of the call if the respondent feels that the purpose of the call does not meet his or her expectations, or that participation in that call does not meet his or her recognized needs. Survey researchers need to understand this to obtain lower refusal rates and accurate information.

In a sense, the history of the telephone, in association with the expansion and diversification of American life, can be represented by a gradual replacement of face-to-face contact by nonvisual, voice-only contact. For many of the same reasons that the telephone has replaced face-to-face contact in business and personal relations, it has done the same in survey research.

Increased Telephone Usage

The contention that the use of telephone surveys will increase or become more popular can no longer be regarded as fanciful projection. For a variety of reasons, some of which will be discussed below, the telephone survey has come of age. While it has not replaced mail and face-to-face surveys, the telephone survey can at least be accorded a place as an equal partner with other methods. The rise of telephone surveys to a position of higher regard in the survey research triad has not come without some resistance, however.

Until recently, data from telephone surveys have been considered suspect, particularly by the academic community. In fact, the use of telephone surveys was discouraged in earlier published methodology texts (Parten, 1950; Sellitz et al., 1959; Kerlinger, 1965), and this technique remains virtually ignored by many of the contemporary treatises on research methods (Sellitz et al., 1976; Babbie, 1979; Backstrom and Hursh-Cesar, 1981). In addition, research scholars were not using telephone surveys. A content analysis of ten major sociology journals for the period from 1960 to 1970 revealed only a handful of surveys that depended on the telephone as a data-collecting technique (Dillman et al., 1976). It was not until the 1970s that marketing research fully recognized the value of using the telephone method over other types of data-gathering (Kegeles et al., 1969).

A large portion of the resistance to the use of the telephone comes not only from tradition, but also from an unfavorable association with the famous *Literary Digest* survey debacle of 1936. It is apparent that this flawed example of survey research remains a millstone around the telephone researcher's neck. To demonstrate the popular diffusion of the image of telephone surveys created by the *Literary Digest* experience, even the most unsophisticated man-in-the-street methodologist will make reference to the 1936 experience when the suggestion of a telephone survey enters the conversation. It is well known that the *Literary Digest* predicted a landslide victory for Landon over Roosevelt in the 1936 presidential race. The sampling frames for this poll, which was a mail ballot, were telephone directories and automobile registration lists, both of which were biased to upper-income groups (Katz and Cantril, 1937). At that time, less than 40 percent of American households had phones, and 55 percent owned automobiles. In addition, mail ballots are more likely to be returned by upper-income groups (Simon, 1978). Not only was the sample skewed to the wealthy, who also tended to be Republicans (and therefore Landon voters), but the *Digest* also included advertising material with the ballot to attract new subscribers. This certainly detracted from the intent of the poll and may have worked against obtaining a higher response rate. Finally, a small response rate of 24 percent was achieved on a mail-out of 10 million ballots. Evidently, the *Digest* pollsters felt that representativeness would be achieved by virtue of the sheer size of the sample. Obviously, this was not the case (Katz and Cantril, 1937: 159). Needless to say, the *Digest* poll exhibited the largest error factor of all the polls conducted for that election. I only elaborate on this particular experience because it illustrates the criticisms that subsequent researchers were able to assign to telephone surveys—namely, inadequate sampling frames and an inadequate distribution of telephones among the population—even though the *Digest* poll was not a telephone survey per se. Other polls predicted the election correctly, but their results have been virtually ignored in accounts of polling history.

A damaged reputation—unfairly, in this case—was not the only reason that surveys by telephone have been avoided until recently. Social scientists had arrived at the conclusion that face-to-face interviews were the best for producing scientifically reliable and valid data, and the neo-positivist assumption about the role of the researcher held that his or her presence would not intrude on the interview process. The scientist was simply a mechanical automaton putting forth questions and "accurately" recording answers presumed to be truthful. Variations in response patterns could not be attributed to the social context of the interview (that is, the race, sex, and/or demeanor of the interviewer, or the interaction of any of the qualities of the interviewer with those of the interviewee). This mechanistic view of research became the normatively supported position within social science and, I might add, marketing communities. Any device that might intrude between a scientist and his or her data source could only compromise data quality, not enhance it.

Of course, the face-to-face interview remains the favorite of many, as old habits are difficult to break. But a number of factors, including cost, time required for completion of research, and compromises in data quality attributable to the social context of the interview, have forced many to abandon, albeit reluctantly, face-to-face methods for the alternative: the telephone survey. Thus, the 1970s saw the telephone break a long-established tradition in data gathering; it would move from a "support" status in relation to other types of surveys to a position where it would be used directly in data gathering.

SUPPORT USES OF THE TELEPHONE

A comprehensive review of the limited number of studies reporting on the improvement of the telephone data-collection method reveals that until recently the telephone had rarely been used as a sole technique for gathering data. The general pattern has been to use the telephone in combination with the mail or face-to-face interview technique and usually for purposes other than gathering information from respondents.

Several researchers have shown that the telephone is a very effective means of prodding nonrespondents to return mail questionnaires (Suchman and McCandless, 1940; Reid, 1942; Donald, 1960; Sudman, 1966; Siemiatycki, 1979). Two studies found the telephone to be equally effective as mail follow-ups, and nearly as effective as sending interviewers to people's homes (Sudman, 1966; Siemiatycki, 1979). The obvious cost advantages of phone interviews over personal visits as a means of follow-up suggest that the importance of the telephone in this capacity is likely to increase.

The telephone has also been used to arrange for personal interviews. Some have credited the telephone with increasing both the probability of completing an interview and the efficiency of doing so, with the latter being due to the necessity for fewer call-backs (Slocum et al., 1956; Sudman, 1966). In contrast, Brunner and Carroll (1967) found that response rates for face-to-face interviews were lower among the group of persons phoned in advance to make interview appointments. Their conclusion, that it is easier to refuse an interview over the phone than it is in person, is one often cited as a weakness in using the telephone method to conduct interviews.

The telephone has also been utilized as a less costly device to screen for rare or highly specialized populations who are to be interviewed in a face-to-face situation at a later time. Sudman (1966) was successful with this technique in locating visually impaired persons in a metropolitan area at one-third the cost of doing the same by personal contact.[1]

Similarly, the telephone has been used to provide advance notice of mail questionnaires. In this capacity, it has not only been found to increase response (Waisanen, 1954; Jolson, 1977), but also to be more effective than the frequently used prior letter (Stafford, 1966). In one study, the use of a short interview by telephone which ended with a request to complete a mail questionnaire did not result in an increased response, but did secure a more rapid return. In all, 80 percent of those interviewed by telephone and who eventually returned the questionnaire had done so prior to the second of three follow-ups, compared to 52 percent in the corresponding group not interviewed by telephone (Dillman and Frey, 1974). In connection with mail surveys, the telephone has been used to determine what portion of nonresponse was due to the inability of the questionnaire to be delivered to the respondent.

Although a number of studies report the use of telephones in a direct capacity to interview respondents, many of them represent cases in which respondents were being resurveyed or where the telephone was being used as a last resort because the respondent had not as yet returned a completed mail questionnaire.[2] Longitudinal surveys of this nature represent a situation in which geographical dispersion typically presents a difficult problem. In such resurveys by phone, response rates of from 84 to 100 percent have been reported (Slocum et al., 1956; Goldberg et al., 1959; Coombs and Freedman, 1964; Kegeles et al., 1969). Sewell and Shah (1968) reported a response rate of 87 percent after three waves of a mail questionnaire and a final telephone interview. One effort to compare the efficacy of follow-up surveys by both mail and telephone showed that the telephone was more effective in raising the response rate. Payne (1964) discovered that mail returns were received from 82 percent of the follow-up respondents versus 90 percent who responded favorably to a telephone call-back.

The versatility of the telephone as a support device to other types of data collection has been established. It continues to play this role. However, the telephone's importance to survey research now rests with its independent use as a data-gathering device. Several factors have contributed to this status change.

FACTORS CONTRIBUTING TO THE INCREASED
USE OF TELEPHONE SURVEY TECHNIQUES

One no longer needs to apologize for choosing the telephone survey as a data-collection mode. There are a number of factors which have contributed to this acceptance.

(1) *The widespread distribution of telephones.* In 1936, the date of the *Literary Digest* poll, only 36 percent of America's households had telephones. These households represented the upper-income portions of the population. Today, approximately 98 percent of all households have phones (U.S. Bureau of the Census, 1981). This figure does vary by region and state, but only five states have less than 90 percent coverage. The portion without phones in any area probably represents those we might call "hard-core isolates"; they could not be reached by any method, whether it be mail, telephone, or face-to-face. Thus, more than ever before, it is possible to obtain a representative sample for a telephone survey, providing a researcher has access to the numbers. In fact, a sample taken for

the telephone may be more precise than a cluster-based area probability sample used for face-to-face surveys (Beza, 1981). Access to a representative sample has been enhanced by recently developed techniques of Random Digit Dialing (RDD), which make it possible to include each member of the population in the sample without having to depend on a sampling frame containing a complete list of potential respondents.

(2) *The development of a wide array of research on all aspects of conducting telephone surveys.* Since the mid-1950s, marketing and social science researchers have been investigating the telephone survey technique. Data are available on refusal rates, interviewing techniques, question complexity, research designs, questionnaire construction, question writing, sampling techniques, and survey design. The Social Research Center of the University of Michigan recently completed an ambitious project to evaluate telephone methods as they compared to face-to-face surveys (Groves and Kahn, 1979). This research, and a good portion of similar projects, developed out of the realization that many of the survey techniques associated with the face-to-face interview are not readily transferable to telephone surveys. Yet a great deal of what is projected as appropriate survey methodology is based on the analysis of experiences with face-to-face interviews. Research on telephone techniques had demonstrated that collecting data by phone requires a significant reorganization of research, particularly in the sampling and data-collection phases.

One of the most significant examples of the development of telephone survey research is found in Dillman's (1978) work on mail and telephone surveys. In this publication, Dillman advocates an approach to conducting surveys which he titles "The Total Design Method" (TDM). This method combines the principles of exchange theory with those of management and administration to produce well-conceived and systematic telephone surveys with high response rates and accurate data within an acceptable time frame. Few details of telephone research go untouched in this work. This, and evaluations like it, has enhanced the data-collection status of telephone surveys by augmenting their operational sophistication.

(3) *Lowered acceptance of traditional methods: the face-to-face interview.* Details of the comparison of telephone surveys with face-to-face interviews will be presented in the next chapter. Suffice it to say that survey researchers were forced to look for an alternative

data-gathering methodology because the traditional face-to-face approach was experiencing some difficulty. The usually high response rates were falling, field costs were rising, and interviewers were reluctant to go out at certain times of the day or to certain locations (American Statistical Association, 1974). It was also becoming increasingly difficult to obtain interviews from those sampled (Groves and Kahn, 1979), because selected respondents were often difficult to locate. Once located, the probability of a refusal was high, and even if the interview was started, it was more difficult to complete. In addition, research was demonstrating that the social context or "demand" characteristics of the personal interview were adversely affecting data quality (for example, social desirability in answers). The telephone survey offered an alternative that was less demanding on resources, though no less complex, but that could produce data of equal or higher quality than those generated in the traditional face-to-face interview.

(4) *Developments in telephone technology and telephone interview technology.* Improvements in telephone technology have contributed to the ease with which calls can be made, particularly long distance calls. Wide-area telephone service (WATS) permits long distance calls to be made with relative ease and at a cost two-thirds of the normal rate. The quality of phone transmission has improved to the point that conversations are less likely to be interrupted by static or disconnection. Even the change from dial to push-button number selection procedures has reduced interviewer fatigue and increased the speed by which calls can be made. Quality control has been enhanced by the ability to utilize a listening device to monitor interviews conducted from the centralized setting.

Perhaps the most significant improvement in telephone interviewing technology has been the development of Computer-Assisted Telephone Interviewing (CATI). All facets of telephone interviewing, including respondent selection, question rotation, response recording, coding data, and monitoring interviewers, are conducted with the assistance of a CRT display and a computer support system. A CATI system, to be described in greater detail in Chapter 5, is expensive to install but saves on time, money, and data quality in the long run. Many of the major commercial and academic survey centers are converting to these systems.

(5) *Complex world requires immediate data retrieval.* Improvements in telephone technology and the administration of telephone surveys

have permitted the almost immediate retrieval of information. A Washington, D.C. pollster employed by former President Richard Nixon could complete a national survey in one night in response to an event that had occurred earlier in the day. The public has become fascinated with political polls that report a candidate's standing almost immediately after he or she has drawn public attention for a certain remark or behavior. Policymakers who are in the daily throes of decision making and program formulation desire feedback from relevant constituencies. Often, they cannot take the time—usually months—to wait for the results of a mail or face-to-face survey. Complexity promotes the need for immediate information feedback; the telephone survey is often the answer.

Plan of the Book

The next chapter compares the telephone survey with the mail and face-to-face methods on several dimensions. The purpose of this section is not to define which is the *best* method, but to assist the researcher in selecting the *most appropriate* technique given his or her problem, resources, and timetable. Chapter 3 discusses the various sampling procedures that are available to those who would utilize a telephone survey. Questionnaire construction is the subject of Chapter 4. The problems of question wording and question order receive the most attention in this section. Chapter 5 outlines procedures for the administration and implementation of a telephone survey. This section includes a thorough description of Computer-Assisted Telephone Interviewing (CATI). The final chapter discusses ethical issues associated with telephone surveys and elaborates on the future prospects for telephone interviewing.

Notes

1. Working from a smaller sample selected by random digit dialing, Hauck and Cox (1974) screened respondents to obtain the household information necessary to select a smaller, specialized sample for follow-up face-to-face interviews. The authors estimated a saving of nearly six dollars per completed interview by using the

telephone rather than additional face-to-face interviews to screen the desired population.

2. Sosdian and Sharp (1980) discovered that despite a first-class mailing, the post office does not always forward mail. As a result of their interviews by phone, they concluded that respondent resistance is not as great a problem in obtaining a satisfactory response rate to a mail questionnaire as is access to the respondent.

CHAPTER 2

COMPARING SURVEY METHODS

Making comparisons of survey methods by specifying the advantages and disadvantages of each or by rating them on some scale of achievement difficulty or "goodness" is risky at best. Few researchers are able to report on experiences with all three methods, as most studies utilize only one form of survey research. The problem of drawing comparisons is further complicated by the fact that reports of surveys rarely contain the details necessary for a complete comparative assessment. For example, information on costs, response rates, administrative arrangements, sampling calculations, and questionnaire formats is not generally included when someone reports their research results. Finally, the methodological comparisons that can be found in the literature, such as Hochstim (1967), Groves and Kahn (1979), and Siemiatycki (1979), are often based on research situations that are unique or that do not seem to duplicate those facing the researcher who must make a data-gathering choice. An additional problem with most of this literature is that only one or a few dimensions (for example, response rate, follow-up procedure, and question order) are compared. As a result, we cannot be sure that all or even a portion of the variation in reported results is not due to unreported research project factors.

Still, choosing the most appropriate survey technique poses an important dilemma, and a summary of comparative advantages and disadvantages can be helpful, if only an "ideal" source of guidelines. Naturally, the research design, including the data-gathering phase, depends on the nature of the problem being studied, the nature of the population being researched, and the extent of the resources available. Certainly, studying the participation of prostitutes in other types of crime calls for a different data-gathering technique than does research on the attitudes of physicians to advertising. A national survey of the voting patterns of the general public calls for different sampling and research design decisions than does a survey of the residents of an apartment complex.

The researcher is motivated by a desire to conduct the best possible study that can be designed for the problem at hand. However, limitations imposed by the time frame, available monetary resources, equipment required, and other factors may force the researcher to "compromise" on his or her "ideal" choice. Such compromises do not have to mean that a less-than-adequate study will be conducted. They only mean that some factors will not be as fully implemented as desired, though attention to the tenets of good research will still be retained.

At one time, it was easier to make a choice of survey techniques because developments in the mail and telephone methodologies had not become very sophisticated (Dillman, 1978). Thus, it was either the face-to-face approach or none at all.[1] Tradition and developments in face-to-face survey procedures supported this choice, as did the well-known fact that the other survey techniques suffered from problems in sample coverage and response patterns (for example, only the well-to-do had phones). Thus, choosing a data-gathering alternative to the face-to-face interview would result in an even greater compromise of one's research objective. Many of these earlier problems associated with mail and telephone surveys, however, have been overcome by developments in sampling procedure, such as random digit dialing, questionnaire construction, and population accessibility. Furthermore, at the same time that problems associated with mail and telephone surveys were being reduced, survey researchers were taking a closer look at the assumptions and procedures associated with the face-to-face survey. As the result of this systematic review, they realized that this technique contained some very apparent detractions, particularly as these concerned response error.

These conditions suggest that the survey researcher is faced with a real and difficult choice on survey techniques. The following compares the telephone technique with mail and face-to-face data gathering on a number of survey dimensions. The purpose is not to reach a decision as to which is "best," but to specify the conditions under which the telephone survey is most appropriate.

Administrative Factors

COSTS

Cost comparisons among survey techniques are difficult to make because costs are rarely reported with research results, and when they are reported, we do not know on what basis they were calculated. For example, overhead or indirect costs are almost never reported and are probably not calculated in cost analyses, particularly for studies done by academicians. Variations in wage rates, telephone charges, supply prices, and sampling expenses also produce cost differentials that are not easily determined.

Three factors seem most significant when costs are calculated—sample size, interview or questionnaire length, and geographic dispersion of sample—regardless of the survey technique. The larger the sample size, the more interviewing hours for telephone and face-to-face surveys, and the more postage or other mailing supplies for a mail survey. There is a point where the marginal cost of adding to the sample size begins to decline, but these costs may still be large, particularly for a face-to-face survey where additional travel and supervisory time must be added to actual interviewing time. Increasing the size of a mail or telephone survey has less of an impact on marginal cost, since call-backs or follow-ups are not as costly.[2]

Interview or questionnaire length also has a significant impact on costs. The mail questionnaire will not suffer increased costs, except where printing charges are raised or if additional length increases the mailing weight to the point where higher postage charges must be paid. Labor charges are not a factor, since it takes the same amount of time to stuff an envelope with a short questionnaire as it does with a lengthier version. Longer interviews do increase field costs in terms of wages and travel time for the face-to-face survey, and data-gathering costs for telephone surveys are similarly affected in terms of wages and supervisory costs.

Cost differentials among mail, telephone, and face-to-face surveys increase as the geographical dispersion of the sample widens. This is particularly true for the costs of face-to-face interviewing; going from a local to a regional or national sample increases dramatically the supervisory, training, and field costs of a face-to-face survey. There is virtually no additional cost to a mail survey utilizing a local, regional, or national sample. Telephone surveys are affected by a dispersed sample with increased phone charges but not in terms of other field costs, such as supervision or follow-up.

Whenever I am contacted about a survey, my first questions are: "What group you are interested in surveying?" "How much are you willing to spend?" and "What are you trying to find out?" I then work backwards by calculating how many persons in the population can be contacted at the established price. I then discuss a fourth question: "How will these data be used?" This is conditioned to a large extent on the nature of the problem and will have an impact on the error rate that will be tolerated. If it is a fairly precise problem requiring that the error rate be low and the completion rate high, the survey will be more costly than a research effort requiring less stringent standards. The final budget is constructed when the decisions on sample size, interview or questionnaire length, and response rate have been made. The limitations presented by the budget will then determine the use of a mail, telephone, or face-to-face survey.

The advantage in a cost analysis goes to the mail survey. The most expensive is the face-to-face, with the telephone survey in between but closer in cost to the mail than the face-to-face survey. The primary advantage of the mail survey is that it is usually less expensive to administer to widely dispersed populations because of standardized postage rates and low labor requirements. Hochstim (1962) reported costs at that time of $10.35 for face-to-face, $6.84 for telephone, and $4.01 for mail surveys. More recently, Dillman (1981) reported that he was experiencing average mail costs of $4.50 and telephone costs of $10-11 per completion. Siemiatycki (1979: 241), in a metropolitan health study, reported rates of $6.08 for mail, $7.10 for telephone, and $16.10 for face-to-face interviews. He also discovered that follow-up by either mail or telephone was less costly than a face-to-face follow-up.

The costliness of the face-to-face survey takes an even more dramatic turn when specifically compared to telephone surveys. In their victimization surveys, Klecka and Tuchfarber (1978) discovered that random digit dialing field work and sampling costs were 15-20 percent lower than those of the face-to-face interview. In the most recent, and most thorough analysis of comparative cost factors, Groves and Kahn (1979) reported that the total direct telephone costs per completion were 45 percent of those using the face-to-face interview. More precisely, for two national samples they show an average cost per telephone completion of $23.45, compared with a face-to-face cost of $54.87. The lower telephone cost was due to the need for fewer supervisory personnel, fewer required materials, lower communication requirements between field staff and interviewers, and little or no travel time by interviewers or supervisors.

Clearly, the cost differentials between the mail and telephone survey and the face-to-face survey are great. This is the major reason that survey researchers are turning to the telephone rather than the face-to-face interview to gather their data. Despite the low cost, the mail survey is not extensively utilized, largely because of the problems of locating an adequate list and of obtaining adequate response rates.

PERSONNEL REQUIREMENTS

If there is any administrative component that has been drastically affected by the switch to telephone surveys, it is that of personnel, particularly as the geographical dispersion of the population being studied widens. The face-to-face survey requires a central staff and field supervisors, a force that must expand as the area to be covered expands; a telephone survey needs only add a few numbers, not people. A local, regional, or even national telephone survey can be conducted with two supervisors and a pool of 12-15 interviewers. A national face-to-face study would require up to 100 interviewers and several supervisors.

In addition, the face-to-face survey requires people who have sufficient social skills to be able to establish a rapport with respondents and who have the time available (for example, daytime hours) to conduct the interviews. They must be able to provide their own transportation and often be willing to work at night—as, of course, must telephone interviewers. Face-to-face interviewers require more extensive training in order to be able to deal independently with sampling and interview situations, anticipated and unanticipated, that may arise in the field. In addition, face-to-face surveys require supervisory personnel who also must be readily available to go into the field to deal with research problems either unanticipated in training or difficult for the interviewer to resolve.

Telephone interviewers typically do not require as extensive skills in independent decision making, since close supervision provided in a centralized location makes it less likely that these interviewers will have to make an independent decision without input from a supervisor. However, this is not to imply that telephone interviewers are less skilled than their face-to-face counterparts. It takes considerable training and experience to be able to persuade a respondent to participate in the interview, to follow what are sometimes very complex orders without breaking the "rhythm" of the interview, and to be able to maintain rapport without the aid of visual cues for what is usually a longer-than-average telephone conversation. At times, telephone interviewing can be even more difficult than the face-to-face variety. The requirements for supervisory positions in a telephone survey are equal to those for a face-to-face interview, since telephone supervisors must be familiar with all of the nuances of the questionnaire, the purposes of the study, and the variation in interviewer style. They must be able to listen to and follow 8-15 interviews simultaneously and to discuss problems quickly when they are encountered. Face-to-face supervisors usually have some time to either consult with their associates or to contemplate a response to an interviewer problem. Telephone supervisors have no such luxury; they must respond immediately to the inquiry. For this reason alone, supervisors should be involved in all preinterview planning and development, particularly with the pretest. Fewer interviewers are needed, as a small crew can complete many interviews in a short period of time. I have seen eight interviewers complete nearly 100 five-minute interviews in a three-hour time frame. Thus, the time per interview for a telephone survey will be considerably less than that of a face-to-face survey.[3]

The mail survey requires almost no personnel trained in research methods. Actually, someone with minimum clerical skills can monitor the mailings, record the returns, and send out follow-up mailings. Therefore, the mail survey is considerably less labor-intensive than either the telephone or face-to-face surveys, with the latter demanding more of labor, both in number and skills, than the telephone survey.

IMPLEMENTATION TIME

Very often a researcher will be called on to conduct a survey within a very constricted time frame, say 4-6 weeks. This time limit could be imposed by a contract or fiscal deadline, by the desire to complete a survey before the occurrence of a major event that could skew responses (for example, an election or a presidential announcement), or because the research is part of a field experiment, with the event as the treatment.

When time is a consideration, the telephone survey is by far the most advantageous, even with a national sample. Mail surveys generally take 3-4 months to complete (that is, to obtain an acceptable response rate), and face-to-face surveys may take at least that long. Recruiting and training personnel, locating respondents, following up on nonresponses, and other organizational arrangements call for a lengthier timetable in face-to-face surveys. Thus, face-to-face and mail surveys, if they have any defined follow-up, are locked into that schedule and must wait for sufficient returns before data analysis can begin (Dillman, 1978).

On the other hand, once a telephone survey questionnaire is developed (and that may not take much time if it is short), data gathering and analysis may take only a few days, or at most a couple of weeks. It is said that President Nixon had a polling firm on call so that he could gauge public response to a pronouncement only a day after it was made. This is the era of the "instant poll" in which organizations can obtain feedback almost immediately to their public actions; this type of poll is almost always of the telephone variety. Speed of completion is an attraction of telephone surveys, but too often a "quick" survey is only possible if the response rate is lower than what should be accepted, or if violations of good sampling principles have occurred. Even though it does take less time to complete a telephone survey, speed should not compromise data quality.

By coding questionnaires as soon as they are completed, by preparing the computer program prior to the completion of the calling, and by keypunching or entering data on a cathode-ray tube (CRT) as recorded, a researcher can have frequency distributions within hours after the last call. Computer-Assisted Telephone Interviewing (CATI) makes this an even greater advantage, provided the software is defined and working (see Chapter 5).

In sum, except in the areas of cost and time of implementation, telephone and face-to-face surveys are equally demanding on personnel requirements. Both need personnel of considerable skill and availability. Telephone interviewers need less skill in making independent decisions, while the face-to-face interviewer often has to make decisions in the field, without the assistance of a supervisor. At the same time, telephone interviewers need considerably more persuasive and conversational skills, since they are only in the verbal presence of the respondent and cannot depend on any additional visual cues to assist them in obtaining and completing the interview. Telephone supervisors are in an especially demanding position, since they must be prepared to respond immediately to respondent inquiries, whereas face-to-face supervisors usually have time to contemplate their responses. The major personnel disadvantage of the face-to-face survey is the increased size of the research staff required to carry out such a project. This, of course, complicates the supervisory task and makes the face-to-face survey more costly than the other types of surveys.

Getting a Representative Sample

SAMPLE COVERAGE

The greater the coverage (the ability to reach all eligible respondents) permitted by a survey, the more valid the results, because more representative samples are possible. Every member of a potential population who is known or reachable should have an equal chance of being selected for a sample. This would not be the case if the location of a respondent could not be determined.

Each survey method has its peculiar problems associated with respondent location and subsequent availability for selection. Until recently, the most prominent criticism of telephone survey coverage had to do with the unavailability of a sampling frame or list containing a complete enumeration of those who were assigned phone numbers. The basic problem was that a list (for example, the telephone directory) does not contain unlisted numbers, new numbers, or recently changed numbers. The development of random digit dialing has virtually eliminated this criticism. The other coverage problem for telephone surveys is that those without phones—nonsubscribers—cannot be included in the sample. The latter is especially a problem in rural and inner-city areas. While we have little information on the characteristics of nonsubscribers, what we do know suggests that these persons are predictably unattached, young members of minorities, and renters (Tull and Albaum, 1977). However, even this is less of a problem than it was ten years ago, since the United States has more phones per 100 persons than any other country in the world (outside of Monaco) and since the household coverage in America has reached over 96 percent—well above the 1970 figure of 83 percent (U.S. Bureau of the Census, 1981).

With well over 90 percent of all households reachable by phone, the sample coverage of the telephone approaches that of face-to-face surveys, which depend on area probability samples. The area probability sample was developed to contain a built-in clustering procedure that made it possible to group interviews and reduce field costs. Most area probability samples are inclusive of at least 95 percent of all local households. However, there are still those "floaters" who are not permanently located and for whom even a temporary address cannot be determined (Groves and Kahn, 1979). Hence, just as the telephone survey faces the difficulty of not being able to reach those without phones, the face-to-face survey has a similar problem with those who lack a permanent residence. If this value does not exceed 3-5 percent of the population, then we can probably assume that any bias as a result of their omission will be small. However, for the study of some subpopulations, such as the poor and elderly, accounting for households without phones is very important.

The problems of changing numbers, temporary disconnects, and a sort of transiency in telephone numbers make the coverage of the face-to-face survey slightly better than that of the telephone (Groves and Kahn, 1979). However, since travel costs are elminiated with telephone designs, it is not necessary to cluster potential respondents. Thus it is possible to contact each individual in a population by telephone at a lower cost and, as a result, the telephone sample will be more pure or representative than the area probability sample, which depends on clustering sample units. Mail surveys have approximately the same potential for coverage as the telephone variety, since it is also possible to identify all dwelling or sampling units.

Mail surveys permit wide coverage at reduced costs, in addition to providing contact with respondents who are difficult to locate and interview by the face-to-face method. Unfortunately, the coverage factor for mail surveys is compromised by the quality of available lists more so than either of the other techniques. In some cases it is possible to utilize a list to generate an area probability sample for a mail survey, but this is rarely done and is only possible if the household is the relevant sampling unit. The result would reflect biases similar to those of the face-to-face sample. The potential for coverage is excellent, with the mail survey, because everyone has a potential address and is, therefore, locatable. In reality, the coverage is somewhat less than desirable because of the mobility of respondents and the unavailability of an adequate list. If, however, the researcher does not expect to generalize his or her results, then representativeness is not necessarily a consideration and a deficient list could be used for a mail sample.

Complete lists of the general public or large heterogeneous samples are not available, and the lists that do exist suffer from several flaws. They may not include every person, either because the enumeration was out-of-date or incomplete (because some people chose not to be on the list, as in the case of unlisted phone numbers), or because they were overlooked by the enumerators. In some cases persons may be listed more than once and thus have a better chance than others for selection. For example, many households have two or more telephone lines or register more than one automobile. In addition, household ownership lists exclude renters and include those who own several homes. Finally, even if a good list were available, getting the list from the owner may be a problem. Thus, mail coverage for the general population is often restricted to available and often inadequate lists, while telephone and face-to-face household surveys can sample without such dependence.[4] Where complete lists are available for homogeneous populations, representatives as provided by coverage is possible for each of the three methods.

RESPONSE RATES–GENERAL PUBLIC

One of the major problems in determining the actual response rate for a survey is to arrive at an agreement on how this rate is to be calculated. This rate should reflect the degree to which a researcher is successful in obtaining cooperation from all potential respondents within a sample (Kviz, 1977). The rate can be calculated as:

$$\text{Response rate} = \frac{\text{Number of completed interviews/questionnaires}}{\text{Number of eligible respondents}}$$

This formula has gained some acceptance among survey researchers (Kviz, 1977; Sosdian and Sharp, 1980). Eligible respondents not only include refusals, but also those who were eligible but who could not speak the language, who were ill at the time of contact, or who could not be contacted but were known to be reachable at a sample's address or phone station. The numerator obviously does not include partial completions; these are calculated as part of the denominator in the equation. This rate is not to be confused with the completion rate, which is generally considered as the proportion of all potential respondents, eligible or not:

$$\text{Completion rate} = \frac{\text{Number of completed interviews/questionnaires}}{\text{Sample size}}$$

The denominator in this formula reflects the figure determined as the result of the size of permitted sampling error. The difference between the response rate and the completion rate is the difference between eligible and ineligible respondents. These rates are quite different, and reported rates must distinguish the basis on which they are calculated.

An additional complicating factor in reporting response or completion rates is the extent to which substitution is permitted. Proper sampling technique suggests that substitution (for example, in place of a refusal by someone originally selected) should not be done, as it may not reflect the characteristics of the original respondent, thereby increasing the potential for response bias and sampling error. Many research firms, academic and commercial, are able to "pad" their response rates by employing an unreported substitution procedure. As a result, their sampling effectiveness and image look better than they otherwise might. Instead, *all* research firms should realistically accept the fact that all eligible respondents are not going to be accessible and report response and completion rates that do not reflect substitution.

In general, we still find response rates for the face-to-face survey to be higher than those for telephone and mail surveys, although the gap is not as pronounced as in past years. This is reflected in the most recent literature. Groves and Kahn (1979) reported a response rate for their national telephone samples of 70.4 percent and of 74.3 percent for the face-to-face surveys. These rates were generally consistent with those obtained by studies conducted by the Survey Research Center at Michigan. In both cases, all categories of nonresponse were higher for metropolitan areas. When comparing the response rates for all three methods, Siemiatycki (1979: 241), using a regional sample, produced initial rates of 70.3 percent for mail, 73.5 percent for telephone, and 84.1 percent for face-to-face. Subsequent follow-ups to the mail and telephone surveys pushed these rates to equal or exceed that of the face-to-face. Dillman (1978: 51) provides ample evidence for a similar distribution of rates. Utilizing his TDM approach, mail response rates for general public surveys ranged from 60 to 70 percent, depending on the extent of follow-up; his telephone surveys obtained rates of 80-85 percent. He projects these to be somewhat lower than what could be obtained in a face-to-face situation.

As indicated above, comparing response rates is difficult because of the unstandardized methods of their calculation. It still appears that mail surveys are obtaining lower (but not unreasonable) response rates than either telephone or face-to-face. In general, it seems that response rates for general public surveys are on the decline, regardless of method, but that the rates for homogeneous samples are still at high levels.

REFUSAL RATES

It is more informative to discuss responses to surveys in terms of refusals, since this component seems to make up the greatest portion of nonresponses to surveys. In addition, most efforts to enhance response rates, short of the less desirable tactic of substitution, are aimed at reducing refusals.

The refusal rate is defined as the proportion of eligible respondents contacted who decline to be interviewed. This would include persons who turn down the interview before, during, or within the first two questions of the introduction to the survey instrument. Obviously, one cannot determine just when the recipient of a mail questionnaire decided not to participate, since it is possible that the mailing was tossed into the garbage before it was even opened, or that the respondent decided not to continue his or her participation even after completing many of the questions. Refusals for telephone and face-to-face surveys can be determined and usually occur during the introductory comments or just before the first question (Dillman et al., 1976).

Refusal rates for mail surveys are difficult to establish because of the inability to sort out intentional nonresponses from those due to undelivered or lost mail. As a result, researchers have done considerable work on stimulating returns in order to bring up the response rate from respondents who do receive the questionnaire. Heberlein and Baumgartner (1978) have identified 71 factors, including personalization, first-class postage, and color of stationery, that have been used in studies designed to stimulate responses. The conclusions are mixed, but follow-up appeals seem to be the most consistent factor in pushing up responses or reducing refusals. In the final analysis, it is much easier to refuse to participate in a mail survey, because the researcher has no control over the respondent's reaction. A

representative of the research is not present, as is the interviewer in telephone and face-to-face surveys, to either persuade
the respondent to participate or to make it appear socially
undesirable to refuse.

Refusals of telephone interviews have been the subject of
some, specific research, though not a great deal. However,
refusal rates are often reported. Wiseman and McDonald
(1979:482) reviewed 182 studies utilizing telephone interviews
and were able to calculate a median refusal rate of 28 percent.
In most cases, this rate was reduced when call-back appointments were made, but efforts to convert refusals produced
unappreciable results. This rate did not vary by length of
questionnaire, survey topic, or geographical location of respondents. In a review of consumer and election surveys from 1953
to 1979, Steeh (1981: 54) determined that refusal rates for
telephone surveys had stabilized at 24 percent. Groves and
Kahn (1979) reported a refusal rate of 28 percent on their
telephone studies, or about 5 percent lower than what was
expected for face-to-face surveys. My own experience with
several metropolitan and statewide surveys is consistent, in that
I have obtained initial refusal rates averaging 20-25 percent.
Refusal conversion efforts resulted in reducing this rate by 2-3
percent. These rates seem to be slightly better than those
obtained in face-to-face interviews, particularly when the latter
are conducted in urban settings.

Reasons for refusal are difficult to determine, especially since
it has been established that most respondents neither resist
surveys as an invasion of privacy nor have had bad experiences
with surveys (Groves and Kahn, 1979; DeMaio, 1980). It is
probably the case that completing a questionnaire or taking the
time for an interview does not have a high priority with the
public. Therefore, it does not take much of a diversion to
replace any interest in survey research participation.

The major problem is to be able to determine the characteristics of refusals in order to compare these to the characteristics
of those who respond. If the differences are great, then bias is
present. Assessment of the characteristics of nonrespondents to

face-to-face surveys is possible because of the ability to note visually certain traits of person and location. Some clues can be obtained in phone surveys (for example, sex, race, and location), but it is virtually impossible to know anything about the characteristics of those who refuse to participate in mail surveys.

NONCONTACT WITH OR LACK OF ACCESSIBILITY OF RESPONDENTS

The portion of nonresponse not attributed to direct refusals from potential respondents is called the *noncontact rate* (NCR). This rate is rarely reported, but it is crucial to understanding the extent to which respondents can be located or are accessible by each method. It is calculated as part of the completion rate:

$$\text{NCR} = \frac{\text{TOTAL not contacted}}{\text{TOTAL known eligibles}}$$

The noncontact rate is considerably lower for face-to-face surveys when the clustering approach includes a quota-block sample rather than a specific household selection sample. Still, the inability to get a response because a respondent is unavailable is one of the more serious factors contributing to the overall lower completion rates that this type of survey is experiencing today. The noncontact rate for face-to-face surveys is compounded by the apparent increased resistance of householders to allowing strangers to enter their homes. Whatever the cause, the rate for face-to-face surveys remains, lower than that of the telephone survey.

The accessibility of respondents is even more of a problem for telephone surveys, particularly where random digit dialing is used. Busy signals, answering machines, disconnected numbers, and no answers inflate this figure. Wiseman and McDonald (1979: 481) noted that for 182 telephone surveys, the median noncontact rate was 39.1 percent. This figure is somewhat inflated, because one cannot be sure that all of the numbers called were working. At least four call-backs could have reduced this rate to 20-25 percent, according to these authors. Of course, these calls can be made at considerably less cost than that of a face-to-face survey.

Again, mail surveys present a dilemma in locating or contacting respondents. On the one hand, the mail survey may be better for hard-to-reach respondents (such as those who are rarely home or those available only after work hours). On the other hand, one cannot know if the questionnaire was received, discarded, lost, or forwarded. Noncontact rates for mail surveys are difficult to determine but may actually be lower than those for either telephone or face-to-face surveys.

ELITE POPULATIONS

The ability to contact prospective respondents who are members of elite populations is one that needs further exploration. What research does exist indicates that elites such as political figures, lawyers, Nobel Prize winners, and so forth are more amenable to interviews in a face-to-face context than by either mail or telephone (Dexter, 1970; Denitch, 1972; Zuckerman, 1972; Becker and Meyers, 1974). Appeals by the latter techniques often end up diverted by "gate-keepers" or others who guard the time and energy of the potential respondent. Those who have done this type of research assert that it is often better just to "appear" at the respondent's office without an appointment and to be prepared to insist on an immediate meeting or an appointment. Once the respondent grants the interview, he or she will usually be very good about answering questions. Apparently, the best role for a mailing and/or a telephone call with these populations is to arrange appointments. As stated above, mail and telephone appeals may be very practical for research on elites, but more information on the best circumstances for using these appeals is needed.

GETTING THE RIGHT RESPONDENT WITHIN A HOUSEHOLD

There are well-known sampling techniques for selecting a designated respondent within a household (see Chapter 3) once contact has been made. However, the problem is complicated by the fact that very often other members of the household will not locate the designated respondent for the interviewer or even allow that respondent to be interviewed. For example, a rather autocratic husband may not allow his wife to be interviewed, or household members will resist attempts to interview an elderly grandparent. In most cases, selection of the respondent can be controlled by the interviewer in telephone and face-to-face situations, and this control can be extended to resisting the motive to substitute respondents, a generally undesirable alternative. It is most difficult, however, to control respondent selection within a household for mail surveys. Even though instructions may specify the desired respondent, it is entirely possible that de facto substitution occurs and that the questionnaire is completed or refused by someone other than the desired respondent.

Data Quality

Obtaining complete and accurate responses from respondents is, of course, the goal of any survey project. There are, however, many factors that can produce responses that are less than complete and that do not reflect the "true" feelings, attitudes, beliefs, or knowledge of the respondent. The occurrence of these types of nonsampling error or measurement effects can be attributed to conditions of the interviewing situation, the response situation, and the questionnaire/interview schedule.

INTERVIEWER EFFECTS–SUPERVISORY CONTROL

The potential for compromises in data quality as a result of interviewer variance is a greater problem for face-to-face surveys than for the telephone survey. Groves and Kahn (1979) found lower interviewer variance in their telephone survey than on the face-to-face component. Interviewer effects are reduced in the telephone survey by virtue of the close supervision provided in a centralized setting. Variations in question order or the manner in which a question is asked can be corrected rather easily in this type of calling facility. The supervisor of an interviewer conducting face-to-face interviews does not have the same control and cannot always prevent interviewers from interjecting their expectations or values into the manner in which they approach a respondent or ask a question. As we shall see in the section on the "social desirability" answering pattern, interviewers contribute significantly to the "demand" characteristics of the interview situation.

Interviewers' effects can be of a relatively subtle nature, or they can be more pronounced. Question wording, instruction guidelines, probing, and questionnaire completion are all factors that can be variously distorted by interviewers. This is particularly the case with a face-to-face interviewer where the survey director is extremely dependent on the field staff. Every once in a while we hear a horror story of how an interviewer completed every one of the assigned interviews in his or her own living room. A centralized telephone facility reduces this source of distortion to a considerable extent because of the ability to monitor the interview. (This can include listening in to both sides.) Validity checks by re-interviews on certain items or by following up with respondents to determine if, in fact, they have been interviewed can reduce this problem to some extent in the face-to-face survey. Even then, this is not infallible, since the resources available for validation are usually only sufficient to permit a small portion of the interviews to be checked.

SOCIALLY DESIRABLE ANSWERS

There is considerable research demonstrating that responses obtained on various items do not accurately reflect respondents' actual views or feelings but rather contain considerable variation due to the "demand" characteristic of the interview situation. These characteristics are usually associated with the influence an interviewer has by virtue of his or her presence and the more subtle influence of the interviewer's expectations and/or characteristics. A respondent's answers may be classified as socially desirable if they seem to be given in reaction to what the respondent feels the interviewer would like to hear or to what the respondent should say if he or she were a spokesperson for one or more groups to which he or she belonged. For example, a respondent might respond favorably to legalizing marijuana because he or she is a teacher and "should be" liberal, even though the person is actually against such legalization.

Recent research has shown that an interviewer's race and ethnicity affect response patterns—that is, produce socially desirable responses, but in a selective fashion. Campbell (1981) determined that race had no general impact on response, except for items related to race. Blacks tended to give "white" responses to these items more so to white interviewers than to black counterparts. These findings corroborate Hatchett and Schuman's (1975-76) work, which also found that a socially desirable response in terms of a deference bias was more likely to occur in mixed-race than consistent-race face-to-face interview situations. In addition, Weeks and Moore (1981) found the ethnicity of the interviewer not to be a factor in response to nonsensitive items but the cause of some differences on sensitive questions.

Most of the literature shows that differences among methods on the rates of socially desirable answers do not vary greatly. However, the general pattern seems to show that mail surveys elicit the lowest rates of socially desirable responses and face-to-face interviews the highest (Wiseman, 1972; Rogers, 1976; Groves and Kahn, 1979). These studies verify what survey researchers have known for some time: the more personal the data-gathering mode, the greater the likelihood of lower data quality. The problem is that we do not know which specific factors are responsible for the differences.

INTERVIEWER EFFECT—ITEM NONRESPONSE

Recent research demonstrates that even with a very structured training program, interviewers will exhibit considerable variability in their data collection, particularly on certain items. Much of this variability is due to the interviewer's expectations for the interview. Sudman et al. (1977) demonstrated that those interviewers who expected difficulties in administering a questionnaire obtained higher item nonresponse rates than those who did not expect any difficulty. Overall, however, response rates were not affected by these expectations. A replication of this study produced similar results (Singer and Kohnke-Aquirre, 1979). However, both Bailer et al. (1977) and Singer and Kohnke-Aquirre (1977) found that a higher nonresponse rate to the income question in a face-to-face survey was obtained from interviewers who thought it inappropriate to ask this item. Even though these authors concluded that their data show only modest effects for interviewer expectations, it is well not to disregard this factor in preparing for a survey.

Interviewer effects on responses should be reduced when examiners are removed from the face-to-face situation and placed in a telephone facility, which permits only vocal cues. It is more difficult to detect interviewer features or preferences in a telephone survey situation that are easily discernible in a face-to-face interview. Still, the personality of the interviewer can have an effect on responses, even in a telephone interview. Rogers (1976) determined that "warm" or more personable interviewers produced higher item nonresponse rates than did interviewers who could be judged as "cool" or task-oriented in their interviewing style. These differences were more pronounced in the face-to-face situation than in the telephone interview (Rogers, 1976: 65)

In general, interviews over the phone and face-to-face do not show significant differences on most items, such as respondent demographics (Rogers, 1976; Groves and Kahn, 1979; Jordan et al., 1980). However, the telephone tends to produce more missing data on the sensitive income item than the face-to-face interview. Groves and Kahn (1979), who experienced this pattern in their national surveys, asserted that over time this difference was reduced by improved telephone interviewing and better supervision in the centralized setting. Finally, Siemiatycki (1979) reported no difference on missing data among the three methods on nonsensitive items, but on the sensitive questions, the mail questionnaire produced lower item nonresponse rates than did the telephone or face-to-face interviews.

QUESTIONNAIRE LENGTH

Length can be defined in a number of ways: number of questions, number of responses required, and of course the length of time it takes to complete an interview or questionnaire. The advantage on this factor still seems to rest with the face-to-face interview, where it is not uncommon to obtain interviews of 60-90 minutes in length. Over the longer interview time, questioners can probe in greater depth, go further in establishing rapport, and thus be in a better position to ask sensitive questions.

For a long time, telephone interviews were criticized because of the apparent inability to conduct rather lengthy interviews over the phone (Simon, 1978). This detraction is less of a problem today than in the past, however, particularly with the development of new telephone techniques in the areas of questionnaire construction and interviewing procedure. Colombotos (1969) successfully interviewed a specialized population of physicians over the phone for an average of 50 minutes. Rogers (1976) reported no problems with conducting the same length interview with the general public of a metropolitan city. Dillman (1978: 55), utilizing his TDM technique, reported few terminations with telephone interviews lasting 20 minutes on the average. Jordan et al. (1980) also report no unusual problems (such as terminations or higher item nonresponse rates) with lengthier telephone interviews. This development is significant because with the rising costs of face-to-face interviews, the ability to get large amounts of information over the phone makes this technique very attractive.

Mail surveys can also be attractive from a financial point of view if length is not a serious drawback. Heberlein and Baumgartner (1978) showed no relation between the length of a mail questionnaire and response rate on the first mailing, but did find a negative correlation on subsequent mailouts. Dillman

(1978: 55) reported little or no variation on response rates for mail questionnaires up to twelve pages or for those with 125 items or less for either a heterogeneous or homogeneous population. There was a negative effect for questionnaires that exceeded these limits.

ANONYMITY/CONFIDENTIALITY

The assurance of confidentiality or anonymity is not always easy to sell these days. Computers, central data banks, junk mail, and unsolicited invasions of privacy do little to promote a sense of trust. "How did you get my name?" or "How did you get my telephone number?" are often some of the first questions asked during the early stages of a telephone or face-to-face interview. In most interviewing or questionnaire situations, the researcher knows the respondent's name, address, phone number, and/or other identifying information. It is always possible that this information will be included on the completed questionnaire. If an interview or questionnaire is presented as anonymous and there is no apparent identifying information, the respondent may feel greater confidence that his or her replies will not (or cannot) be identified (Simon, 1978), and the respondent may therefore be more truthful in responding. However, since it is virtually impossible to find a research effort where there is absolutely no way to trace a respondent, it is more appropriate to compare the three survey methodologies on the dimensions of confidentiality.

The mail or telephone survey would seem to have the advantage in establishing confidentiality. A confidential response is made by a respondent whose identity is known but kept secret. In the case of the face-to-face survey, more identifiable information is known—name, address, dwelling type, physical appearance, and so forth—than with either mail or telephone surveys. Confidentiality can also be compromised by validation callbacks that tell the respondent that his or her name and some identification information *have* been passed on, if only to the project supervisor.

It is not known how many respondents surveyed by telephone refused to participate because of privacy reasons. However, in random digit dialing surveys, the original identifying information includes only a phone number (it is not necessary to have the respondent's name), which results in greater, but not total, anonymity. If more specific geographical location is necessary to some kind of neighborhood analysis, one never asks for the street address but only for the nearest major intersection or large cross-streets. Directory sampling provides more identifying information and places the telephone survey at a disadvantage in this regard, almost to the extent of the face-to-face survey.

There is very little research on the relation of refusals, premature termination, or other patterns of response to respondent feelings of privacy invasion, loss of anonymity, or distrust of assurances of confidentiality. Edwards (1957) found a higher occurrence of "don't knows" with a face-to-face survey than with a survey by "secret ballot." King (1970), Fuller (1974), and Wildman (1977) found no differences in response rates to mail surveys between respondents who received questionnaires with premailed identification numbers and those without. My own experience suggests that refusal to participate or item response bias comes not as a result of the anonymity/confidentiality issue, but in response to the subject of the survey and the manner in which it is presented. I am continually amazed at the freedom with which people respond to an interview once they agree to participate. In sum, each of the three methods suffers from a general distrust of institutions and from the resultant belief that assurances of confidentiality are difficult to believe. Many respondents probably believe that if someone wanted to trace their responses, he or she could by being sufficiently persistent and/or creative. Their only hope may be that no one will care. In this context, it is foolish even to talk of anonymity, since its guarantee is a virtual impossibility. Perhaps all that survey researchers can hope for is that the quality and reputation of their craft is such that most people will not feel distrust when called upon to respond to a survey.

ASKING SENSITIVE QUESTIONS

Sensitive questions are those that are potentially embarrassing or threatening to respondents. Recalling the earlier maxim that the more personal the method, the less likely to get reliable information, it would seem that the face-to-face interview should elicit more problems with this type of inquiry. Actually, the opposite seems to be the case. Although Hochstim (1967), Wiseman (1972), and Lucas and Adams (1977) reported few or no differences among survey methods on response rates to sensitive items such as income, more recent research suggests that the face-to-face technique obtains lower item nonresponse rates to this type of question.

Groves and Kahn (1979) and Jordan et al. (1980) report more evasiveness and nonsubstantive responses to sensitive items over the telephone than face-to-face. In fact, Groves and Kahn (1979) found a higher proportion of persons surveyed by telephone who resisted responding to these items because they felt uneasy answering a sensitive question. Siemiatycki (1979) found that the mail survey obtained the lowest item non-response rate to sensitive items and the telephone the highest.

AIDING THE RESPONSE–PROBING AND CLARIFICATION

Telephone questionnaire usage has been limited to some degree due to criticism that complex questions or those requiring an in-depth response cannot be asked because they will keep respondents on the phone too long, thereby promoting a premature termination or producing responses that are of lower quality than could be obtained with shorter, less demanding questions. In addition, response quality may be compromised because sufficient assistance in terms of visual aids or clearly communicating cues cannot be given to aid responses. The face-to-face survey is viewed as the one method that does not have these difficulties. Actually, more difficulties exist for asking complex and probing questions in mail surveys than in either of the two interview methods.

COMPLEX QUESTIONS

The advantage here appears to go to the face-to-face interview because of the presence of an interviewer who can verbally clarify any misunderstanding and also offer visual aids (a map, response cards, and so forth) to assist the respondent. In the face-to-face situation, cards can be shown to respondents to aid their selection of an appropriate response category. This allows respondents to avoid giving direct answers and thus increases the validity of responses (Groves and Kahn, 1979). The major problem with clarification in a face-to-face situation is in the process of re-asking the question; the interviewer's bias is less subtle, and on-the-spot rewording can change a question. If "controlled" or "standardized" clarification is not implemented, then question comparability is compromised.

In a mail questionnaire, if a subject misinterprets a question or records his or her response in an uninterpretable manner, there is little that can be done to remedy the situation. A good graphic artist can provide some visual interpretations beyond the simple listing of categories, but again, misinterpretation without clarification is possible. If the respondent feels it necessary to seek clarification of a mail survey question, he or she may go to a friend or family member for consultation. The ramifications of this are obvious—a response that may not reflect the actual feelings of the selected respondent. Consultation with others is virtually impossible with the face-to-face or telephone survey because of the ability of the interviewer to direct response patterns.

There is increasing evidence that complex items can be asked over the phone, even without the assistance of visual aids. Rogers (1976) found no difference in response quality on complex items for both face-to-face and telephone interviews. Still, the problems of clarification discussed with respect to the face-to-face survey prevail. The telephone survey has more difficulty with complex questions, such as those requiring the ranking of several items, than either the mail or face-to-face method. It is encouraging to note, however, that new techniques (particularly CATI) are being developed to overcome this detraction with telephone surveys.

PROBING—OPEN-ENDED ITEMS

The opportunity to probe is not, of course, possible with the mail questionnaire because their is no interviewer present. A less obvious problem with asking open-ended questions (that is, those for which no answer categories are provided) is that they are demanding of the respondent, particularly for one who has difficulty expressing himself or herself in words. It is estimated that nearly 10 percent of the adult population is illiterate. For questionnaires of any complexity, the percentage who could not understand the questions would be even higher; thus, only those with some education could respond. Complicated questionnaires require motivation and patience to write in detail, as well as time and ability (Simon, 1978). This means that one must be very careful in the use of open-ended questions in surveys, particularly mailers.

On the other hand, there is no problem using this type of question with either telephone or face-to-face surveys, although there is some evidence that the telephone elicits shorter, truncated answers (Groves and Kahn, 1979) to open-ended questions. Neither face-to-face nor telephone interviews provide the opportunity for respondents to deliberate on their answers for very long. The presence of the interviewer is one of those "demand" characteristics that may lead respondents to answer sooner than they would like; the result is often a shorter and more superficial response. This problem could be solved with extensive interviewer training on the probing and clarification of responses. Verbosity, not conciseness, can also be a problem when using this type of question in surveys. Interviewers must be trained in how to terminate an answer, as well as how to stimulate one.

Concluding Remarks

Table 2.1 lists the factors on which mail, telephone, and face-to-face surveys compared and their evaluations as advantages or disadvantages for either method. In reviewing this table,

TABLE 2.1   Comparison of Mail, Face-to-Face, and Telephone Survey Methods

Factor	Mail	Face-to-Face	Telephone
1. Cost	1	4	2
2. Personnel requirements: interviewers	N/A	4	3
3. Personnel requirements: supervisors	2	3	4
4. Implementation time	4	4	1
5. Sample coverate	3	1	1
6. Response rate–general public	4	2	2
7. Refusal rate	Unknown	3	3
8. Noncontact/nonaccessibility	2	3	2
9. Ability to obtain response from an elite	4	1	2
10. Respondent within household	4	2	2
11. Interviewer control	N/A	3	1
12. Socially desirable response	1	4	3
13. Item nonresponse	3	2	3
14. Length of questionnaire–impact or response	3	1	2
15. Confidentiality	4	4	4
16. Ability to ask sensitive questions	2	1	2
17. Ability to probe	4	1	2
18. Ability to clarify	4	1	2
19. Ask complex questions	3	1	3
20. Use of open-ended questions	4	1	1
21. Use of visual aids	2	1	4
22. Avoid opportunity for consultation by respondent with others	4	1	1

Key: 1 = Major advantage   3 = Minor disadvantage
       2 = Minor advantage   4 = Major disadvantage

one needs to keep in mind that no survey rises or falls on the implementation or failure to implement any one of these factors. The success or failure of a survey depends on a combination of factors and their interaction. As this list demonstrates, it is also important to point out just how difficult it is to select the appropriate research strategy. Each strategy has its strengths and weaknesses, and each requires careful attention to design and procedure. The telephone survey method cannot be categorically rejected as inferior to the face-to-face approach nor accepted as superior. However, there have been a considerable number of improvements in sampling procedures, questionnaire design, and administrative practice for telephone surveys that make this approach more attractive than ever before. The remaining chapters will outline some of these improvements.

Notes

1. There are several forms of face-to-face interviews. Focused interviews, "free story" interviews, and group interviews are some examples. For the purpose of this chapter, the face-to-face interview will be restricted to a situation where one interviewer administers a relatively structured questionnaire to a single respondent within a limited time period and in the physical presence of the respondent.

In addition, a great deal of the literature on survey research uses face-to-face interviewing interchangeably with "personal interviewing." Actually, the telephone interview can also be considered personal, even though mutual physical presence is not a factor. Verbal communication is sufficient to make an interview "personal." As a result, I prefer to utilize "face-to-face" as a more realistic description of the interview situation that I am comparing to one using the telephone.

2. One has to be careful in a mail survey to calculate an original sample size that will allow for follow-up mailings. I have known researchers to use up their mailing budget on the original mailing, thereby leaving insufficient funds for even a postcard follow-up.

3. Groves and Kahn (1979) reported that 3.3 hours of work were devoted to each telephone completion and 8.7 hours to each face-to-face completion.

4. These problems can also be attributed to lists of specialized populations (for example, students, physicians, and union members). It is not safe to assume that even these lists are up-to-date or accurate, or that one can generalize results based on samples drawn from these lists.

CHAPTER 3

SAMPLING

Today's increased demand for survey data means that greater attention to all facets of survey design, particularly respondent selection, is required. As survey results are being used more and more for precise estimates of population characteristics, rather than predicting "ballpark figures" or "getting a sense" of dispositions, great care must be taken to select respondents in such a fashion that each has the same chance of selection and that sampling error is minimized. The evolution of telephone surveys to a position of quantitative and qualitative prominence in survey research has largely come about as the result of improvements in sampling designs whereby it is now possible to implement probability sampling procedures for even the largest populations (including the general public).

Currently, there is a wide variety of sampling designs in use for telephone surveys. These designs vary in the extent to which they implement probability sampling procedures, depend on random number usage, utilize available lists such as the telephone directory or cross-reference directory, and depend on local telephone companies for information. These designs can be categorized into those that depend on the telephone directory or another available list as a sampling frame and those based on some version of random digit dialing. Actually, all of these designs depend to some extent on the directory, if only to determine the prefixes in use (739, 476, and so forth).[1] However, random digit dialing techniques are distinguished by their selection and assignment of from one to several random digits as substitutes for all or a portion of the directory-listed numbers. All of these designs are based on the tenets of probability sampling, even where a directory is utilized and unlisted numbers are not included; at least each listed number will have an equal chance of selection in these cases. Nonprobability samples are rarely utilized in telephone surveys, except in situations where "call-in" polls are conducted by the news media or radio talk shows, for example. Each of the probability designs currently in use in telephone sampling is discussed below.

Sampling From Lists: Directories and Others

Early sampling designs called for respondent selection from some kind of list, usually the telephone directory or one of the many cross-reference or criss-cross directories. Because of several problems, these directories are rarely used as the sampling frame for a telephone survey, except where it is known that they contain nearly complete population coverage, such as in rural areas. Directory listings are also useful when searching for rare or specialized subsamples (Frankel and Frankel, 1977), when one is interested in sales rather than research and a nonprobability sample is thus acceptable, or when augmenting a random digit dialing survey. Before discussing the directory-based designs, we need to discuss some of the difficulties associated with the use of lists.

PROBLEMS WITH LISTS

Obtaining a List. First, obtaining a list may be problematic. Very often, access to an organization's list of members is restricted by the fact that no one knows who has the most up-to-date version, or by the necessity to get approval to use the list from a special committee, Board of Directors, or key staff person. In each case, delay and/or denial are often the results of a request to use a list. In addition, many lists are protected by privacy provisions that make clearance for survey use virtually impossible to obtain. Finally, most available lists are worthless in that they are out of date, incomplete, or based on other inadequate lists (Sudman, 1976). These problems are compounded if a national sample is the goal and the general population is the target. Any nationwide list of organization members is difficult to assemble, much less keep up to date; and a single list of the general population, or of significant subgroups such as males, whites, or senior citizens, even at the regional or state level, is nonexistent. The best approximation of a national list is, of course, the telephone directories.

Even telephone directories may be difficult to obtain, except in local or state situations, though American Telephone and Telegraph does publish a *Directory of Directories,* which lists all of the operating telephone companies and their jurisdictions. Since any firm that does national sampling must have all of the current directories on file, this source is an asset to the search for these lists. Bell and Howell (1981) also maintains a microfiche file of the telephone directories of approximately 250 metropolitan cities, as well as a cross-reference guide to these cities and their telephone directories. These are updated regularly and can be obtained for a subscription fee. The problem is that microfiche is not easy to work with, and its use can cause unusual operational problems (such as delay or employee fatigue) for the sampling phase of a project. In addition, writing local companies for their latest directory provides no guarantee that the directory will arrive on time or that it will be the most recently published version. Finally, monitoring directory publication for a firm that does regional or national surveys is a task that can keep one person in full-time work, thereby increasing overhead costs.

Ineligible Listings. Any obtained list will contain entries that are not eligible for the survey because they do not fulfill the membership criteria (for example, own a certain car, reside in the appropriate geographical area, are over age or under age, pay dues, and so forth), or because they fulfill membership criteria but represent a subsample that is of no interest to the survey. Where ineligibility is known, as through a commercial listing in a telephone directory, some techniques for substitution can be implemented, such as alternatively selecting the name above or below the ineligible listing. Another eligibility problem associated with telephone directories is that they usually contain exchanges or community listings that are not to be included in the survey. If not separated in advance, an elaborate and costly substitution process must be implemented or geographical eligibility determined with screen questions. In either case, survey costs rise. In addition, since any published telephone directory is three to four months out of date when it is published, it can contain the numbers of persons who have moved from the area and are no longer eligible for the survey. Cooper (1964) noted that directory listings declined by approximately 12 percent over a year; Dillman (1978) estimated an attrition rate of 11-14 percent. This could present serious sampling problems for some studies, as those who move have different characteristics than those who do not move. Sampling efficiency also goes down as more nonworking members are located in the selection process. Finally, where they are unknown, ineligibles can adversely affect sampling selection probabilities by reducing the chance of selecting an eligible respondent, and can push up survey costs because of the resources used in wasted calls.

Duplicate Listings. Units on a list that appear more than once have a greater chance of selection than those that appear only once. This selection bias is ordinarily small but could have serious consequences (Sudman, 1976). Cooper (1964) determined that 3 percent of residential subscribers to a midwest directory had multiple listings of two or more phone numbers for the same address. These were determined to be families at the professional occupational levels. Automobile registration lists often have this same problem with multiple listings, since there are many American families with two cars; some have three or four vehicles.

Duplications can be determined in advance by scrutinizing the list, but this can be an arduous and time-consuming task. Some researchers avoid such a preliminary search by simply asking the question: "How many cars do you own?" or "How many telephones do you have in your household with separate numbers?" Some of the completed interviews could be selectively discarded, but this is a waste of collected data. A better procedure is to weigh the results by the inverse of the probability of selection (Sudman, 1976). Thus, if a sample element were listed three times, it would be weighted by one-third. ' Similar considerations must be given to those who may be listed in more than one directory. Again, this is a small proportion, particularly for residential listings, but when a researcher is working with multiple directories, which is usually the case in large, urban areas, he or she should be aware of the possibility of duplications of listings among directories.

Incomplete Coverage: Omissions. The most serious problem with lists is that a portion of the eligible population, as defined by the research problem, is usually not included. This condition provided the primary impetus for the development of random digit dialing, a sampling technique designed to compensate for the omission of numbers from the directory that are unlisted or recently assigned. In addition, there is the problem of not being able to include in the sample those without phones, or cars, or whatever the basis of the list happens to be.

Since 95-97 percent of the households in America have phones, the omission of those who do not is one that survey researchers have come to regard as not necessarily a serious sampling problem. There is, however, some evidence of differences between those who have phones and those who do not. Leuthold and Scheele (1971), for example, noted that rural, low-income, inner-city nonwhites and those who could be classified as "isolated" tend not to have phones. Still, as stated in the previous chapter, telephone surveys provide coverage that is comparable to that of household surveys, and the proportion not reachable by phone is consistent with the proportion not reachable in household surveys—it is very small. Finally, the pre-interview costs of reaching those without a phone are so high that justifying this effort would be difficult.

The omission of unlisted numbers and new listings from published directories is a more serious consideration, however. Within the American population, the trend to have unlisted numbers has produced estimates of 16-20 percent in some areas

(Glasser and Metzger, 1975; Rich, 1977), and upward to 30 percent in others (Rich, 1977; Frey, 1979). Rich (1977) also noted that the rate of unlisted numbers in urban areas soared 70 percent between 1964 and 1977. Groves and Kahn (1979) reported an unlisted rate of 27 percent for their latest national sample. When you add the new, but unpublished, listings to this figure, it is possible that at any one time, nearly 40 percent of all telephone subscribers could be omitted from the telephone directory. Therefore, any listing which is dependent on the telephone directory for its information will also suffer from this deficiency. There is ample evidence to demonstrate that those with unlisted numbers differ on a number of characteristics from those with published phone numbers. Those with unlisted numbers tend to be younger, have lower incomes, and live in urban areas. They are also nonwhite, nonjoiners, renters, and less educated (Brunner and Brunner, 1971; Roslow and Roslow, 1972; Glasser and Metzger, 1975; Rich, 1977). Obviously, the differences are too significant for those with unlisted numbers to be overlooked in any probability sampling procedure.

"Dirty" Lists. Many lists, including the telephone directory, are what we call "dirty" and need to be "cleaned up" before they can be used. Many of the names on a mailing list contain incorrect addresses or phone numbers. Frequently, the phone number is omitted from the listing, and a time-consuming search must be commenced. Of course, if the address or phone number is unlisted for a selected respondent, extra sources are necessary to trace a number or location for that person. This effort often produces failure. Even the phone directories, which are presumed to be reliable, sometimes contain incorrect listings. The value of this figure has been estimated at 1 percent of all listings for a metropolitan area (Blankenship, 1976).

DIRECTORY SAMPLING TECHNIQUES

Despite the problems noted above, survey researchers will often sample from available lists. It is possible for the sampling frame to be judged as adequate given the nature of the research problem or the characteristics of the population. The list may, for example, contain a significant portion of the population, thereby minimizing the problems associated with incomplete coverage. A recently published directory of professionals (including lawyers and doctors) is an example. At times, using the available listing is the only alternative, particularly for some specialized groups and where limited resources and information prevent screening for a particular subgroup. We recently conducted a survey of musicians utilizing the directory published by the local labor union. Even by using the most recently published version and "cleaning up" the list as much as was possible, we knew that the listing was incomplete and contained inaccurate information in some cases. Still, we proceeded to use this list because of the crunch of a deadline and the lack of funds to develop sampling alternatives or to supplement the directory sampling (for example, by screening the general population for musicians). Finally, a list may be used when generalizing to the larger population is not a serious consideration; perhaps the researcher wants only a "sense" of the feelings or attitudes of the population in question. Thus, a quota or some other nonprobability sampling design could be used. However, I recommend the use of one of the sampling designs described below whenever a list is available and even if nonprobability considerations could possibly apply.

Simple Random Sample (SRS). If a directory is fairly small, it is possible to draw a simple random sample by numbering each name on the list, excluding nonresidential listings and using a table of random numbers to assist the selection. The numbering can be done by counting every name or by working with the average number of listings from a sample of randomly selected pages. For example, if a page averaged 75 names and the random number 320 was selected, the sampling enumerator would page to the fifth page of the directory and count down 20 residential listings from the first such listing on the page. This procedure would be followed until the entire sample had been drawn. Another slightly more efficient way to draw a simple random sample is to follow a two-step sequence of selecting a page and a name from that page by random procedures (Dillman, 1978).

A simple random sample of either type is almost never used. To draw such a sample requires a great deal of enumerator time; it is tedious to number each listing or to make repeated counts to obtain a sampling element. Thus, an SRS is simply not a convenient or efficient sample to draw. This is especially true for regional or national samples, and for samples that depend on any but the simplest sampling frames. Finally, we know from sampling theory that even though simple random sampling is the basis on which statistics related to sampling precision are calculated, this method does not always produce the most accurate sample (Babbie, 1973). Empirically, the results from simple random sampling have been shown to be identical and, in some cases, inferior to results obtained from systematic sampling.

Systematic Sample. Systematic samples call for the selection of every k[th] listing until the desired sample size has been drawn. The initial element is selected by referring to the Table of Random Numbers. This is called a *random start,* and this feature gives the systematic sample its designation as a probability sample. The selection process continues by determining the *sample interval,* or the distance between elements selected for the sample. The interval is calculated by dividing the sample size required into the size of the population to be sampled. Thus, if the list contains 20,000 names and a sample of 500 is desired, the interval would be 40. This type of sample is more convenient and efficient than the simple random sample and is utilized with considerable frequency in telephone survey work. It is readily adaptable to local, regional, or national samples.

Before systematic sampling can be implemented, it is important that the list be examined for "periodicity" or any pattern within the list. Should this pattern coincide with the sampling interval, the equiprobability of selection is compromised, and bias is the result. For example, say our list of 20,000 names represented an organization with a specific local group arrangement. It is possible that every fortieth name would be a group leader or national contact person, and only these persons could be in the systematic sample. Periodicity is not really a danger with alphabetic lists; therefore, sampling from this type of list should be representative of the population portrayed in the list.

There are several procedures that can be followed to implement a systematic sample. These include:

Single Directory Sampling

(1) Determine the size of list and sample size.

(2) Determine the sampling interval (k) by dividing the desired sample size into population size.

(3) Determine a random start by selecting a number from a Table of Random Numbers. Be sure that the size of the random digit is the same as the number of digits in the population size. Thus, if a list contains 20,000 names, the random digit should be five numbers (00248, 17621, and so forth).

(4) Proceed through the list, taking every k^{th} listing from the random start.

(5) If selection is not a residential listing, alternatively take the next preceding or successive listing. Begin the next interval count from the original nonresidential listing; otherwise, any listing at interval's length from this listing would not have a chance for selection.

Multiple Directory Sampling

(1) Acquire all relevant telephone directories.

(2) Determine the sample size.

(3) Determine the size of each directory list. Since it is rather tedious to count all the directory listings, it is permissible to estimate the size of each directory by sampling several pages from it—say, 5-15 pages, depending on the size of the directory—counting the eligible listings on each page, determining an average, and multiplying that average by the total number of pages. Add up the directory totals to determine the population size.

(4) Determine the proportion of the total population represented by each directory. These same proportions should be represented in the sample. That is, if the listings from city A represent 10 percent of the total population of 20,000, or 2,000 names, then city A should make up 10 percent of our sample of 500, or 50 names. The result is a proportionate stratified sample based on geographic location and directory size.

(5) Proceed to draw a systematic sample within each directory as follows:

(a) Determine the sampling interval for each directory. Again, the subpopulation size is divided by the subsample size to determine the interval. For city A's directory, the interval is 2,000/50, or 40.

(b) Determine the random start for each directory.

(c) Select the subsample by taking every k^{th} element from and including the random start listing. If the sampling interval is quite large (for example, 40-80 listings), counting intervals by single listing can be quite time consuming. In this case, it is permissible to obtain an approximate measure of the distance between selected sampling elements. That is, measure the sampling interval by something other than the number of listings. Dillman (1978) suggests using column inches. Excluding large blocks of government and commercial listings, a sample interval of 40 will measure five column inches. Using a ruler, the enumerator simply draws the sample by selecting the random start and measuring five inches to select the next sampling element. Blankenship (1977) suggests the use of a template to make a similar measure. Such devices are utilized more as a matter of convenience than of adherence to any principles of accuracy, although the latter do not seem to be compromised to a great extent by using these measuring devices.

(6) If the interval falls on a nonresidential listing, substitution is made by systematically taking the name above or below the original selection. Where the interval falls on a multiple listing, the residential number is taken only if the interval actually falls on that number. If the interval falls on a listing that requires two lines because of a long name, the residential

number is selected, but counting proceeds from the line on which the original interval fell.

Add-A-Digit Sampling. A third directory-assisted sampling technique calls for the addition of a number between 0 and 9 to the last digit of a selected phone number. The number chosen may be a constant for all numbers, or it may be assigned randomly for each selected number. Thus, under a "plus-one" approach, if the number 456-7824 is selected, the actual number called is 456-7825. This technique represents a rather simple way of including voluntary unlisted numbers or numbers that were added since the directory was published. This technique is not limited to the last digit, as numbers can be added to the last two or three digits as well. The more numbers substituted, the greater the chance of selecting voluntary unlisted numbers or numbers assigned after the directory was published.

Landon and Banks (1977) compared this technique to a random digit dialing (RDD) sample and found the former to be more efficient (that is, fewer wasted calls); it also included a similar portion of new and unlisted numbers. The problem with the add-a-digit technique is that unless the working numbers are assigned in definable groups within banks, leaving large blocks of numbers unassigned, add-a-digit will not improve efficiency. That is, the technique will not catch any more working numbers than one of the other random digit dialing techniques. This is true for digit changes of every size. The smaller the number of digit change (for example, 2 instead of 3 or 4), the more sensitive the sampling to the assignment of new numbers or unlisted numbers. Also, equiprobability of selection is compromised by the add-a-digit technique because in order for a number to be included in a sample, its predecessor must be listed. If a number is not in the directory, this eliminates any chance that the numbers that follow will be in the sample (Landon and Banks, 1977). Conversely, the number following a listed number has a disproportionate chance of selection. This technique would be most appropriate to use where working numbers are clustered into banks (for example, 2000-2999,

4000-4999), telephone directory coverage is extensive, a low percentage of numbers are voluntarily unlisted, and/or new numbers are only infrequently added.

Random Digit Dialing

Random digit dialing (RDD) procedures were developed as a reaction to the problems of undercoverage in telephone directories. It was necessary to develop a technique that would overcome the problems of incomplete, inaccurate, and out-of-date directory listings. The add-a-digit technique described above represents one effort to compensate for the nonpublished bias, but if these numbers are not assigned randomly, selection bias remains. The several random digit dialing techniques are distinguished by their use of random selection and by the substitution of all or a portion of the last four digits of a phone number.

Most varieties of random digit dialing depend to some extent on a directory for information about telephone number assignment. The researcher needs to be able to determine the working three-digit prefixes, the assigned banks of 1000 series and, if using a regional or national sample, the relevant area codes. This information can often be obtained from the local telephone company or from such publications as the AT&T *Long Line Directory* or its *Network Guide*. There are approximately 4,500 telephone directories in the United States, with 130 area codes and over 30,000 central office codes (COC = 739, 248, and so forth). The COCs are found in one exchange only, and these exchanges, as with area codes, do not cross state boundaries. Thus, the arrangement of telephone numbers permits a natural stratification by state and area code for national sampling (Groves and Kahn, 1979). Each COC consists of 10,000 numbers (0000-9999). None of the COCs is completely assigned or filled. Four-digit numbers tend to be assigned in blocks or bundles of 1,000 or 100. There is no apparent system, either random or nonrandom, to the assignment of numbers within COCs or blocks of 100 or 1,000.

Not only do random digit dialing designs provide for the inclusion of unlisted numbers, they have the additional advantage of eliminating the need to list or enumerate units prior to drawing a sample. In addition, not having to list sampling elements reduces the time it takes to implement a random digit dialing survey, as compared to that of a directory-based sample design (O'Neil, 1979). In these days of resource conservation, the subsequent advantages of lower cost, particularly in wages, make the use of random digit techniques even more attractive.

SIMPLE RANDOM DIGIT DIALING

This technique calls for the random assignment of four digits to a selected area code/COC combination. The procedure is as follows:

(1) Define the universe as households with phones, either at the national, regional, or local level.[2]

(2) Sample proportions will be based on the number of residential listings per state, if a national sample. The county or Standard Metropolitan Statistical Area (SMSA) can also provide the basis for sample allocation, depending on the scope of the survey. The assignment of area codes and central office codes can be determined in advance by consulting an available directory or the *Long Line Directory* of AT&T.

(3) Since we do not usually know the number of working residential numbers per COC, prefixes will be selected at random and an equal number of completions assigned to each COC. If the number of residential listings per COC is unknown, then a proportionate stratified sample can be implemented.

(4) Assign a weight (for example, one-half, one-third) to responses from multiple-listing households, depending on the number of different listings in that household.

(5) Screen for geographical coverage if the COC or exchange does not match the survey area; that is, determine that an exchange is located within the survey area. If this cannot be determined, respondents will have to be screened after contact is made.

(6) Random digit numbers are generated for each prefix. Thus, the first number called would be *COC + four-digit random number.*[3] Where working banks (1000 numbers) are unknown, it is wise to draw at least five random numbers for each expected completion. The random creation of seven- or ten-digit numbers is not done because the total number of combinations is many times the actual number of residential listings in use.

(7) Continue calls until the desired number of completions is achieved. Nonworking and noneligible numbers are eliminated in the process.

For national and regional samples, the result is a stratified sample by state or county listings. A local sample would not be stratified unless it were possible to obtain the number of residential phones assigned to each COC or prefix. This information is rarely available, and even if obtainable, its accuracy would be questionable, since number assignment changes on an almost daily basis.

The simple random digit dialing technique is rarely used because of its inefficiency. Under this system, a randomly generated number could be a working household number, a working nonresidential number, or a nonworking number. Since only 20 percent of assigned numbers are residential, and since there are nearly 10 billion working numbers nationwide, the chances of selecting a nonresidential number are great. These numbers can be screened from the sampling procedure only if there is information available about any pattern of assignment to commercial or nonresidential locations (for example, commercial accounts are contained within 1000-3999 banks).

Such information is almost never available, and patterns cannot be discerned from phone directories. Thus, if any improvement in efficiency is to be made, it is in making some determination of the working banks (1000 numbers) of assigned numbers. This means that the most efficient sampling designs make use of both the telephone directory and random number selection. The remainder of the random digit dialing techniques implement this principle.

In response to the inadequacies of sampling from the telephone directories, Cooper (1964) suggested one of the first random digit variations: Instead of using a telephone directory, he chose to use a cross-reference directory to determine the working banks of numbers within each central office code (COC) in use. In addition, he randomized the last three digits, rather than four, of the selected numbers. This technique includes the following strategies:

(1) Locate a criss-cross or cross-reference directory. More than likely, a local university or public library will have at least one of the fifteen or so that are available. Instead of arranging customers by name as to telephone directories, this type of reference arranges entries by street, house number on that street, and by COC, with numerical sequences of numbers. For example, a typical listing in the *Hill-Donnell Reference Directory* looks like this:

Prefix	No.	Name	Address
293			
	2018	Jones, Art	1012 Western Ave.
	2121	Brown, Wm	48 Main St.*
	2249	Smith, George	218 First St.
	3721	Acme Electric	4112 Center St.

Numbers or street addresses are highlighted by some distinguishing mark (such as an asterisk) if they represent new or changed entries since the last directory was published.

Most of these directories are published each year, but the publication date is not always predictable. Also, these directories do not cover all cities, nor do they include all possible listings, since entries are based on published telephone directories. However, their greatest asset may be the sequential list of phone numbers by COC; that certainly makes it possible to determine the approximate range of assigned numbers for each COC and to determine in advance of sampling the prefixes that are essentially business or nonresidential. In addition, this list gives the researcher some idea of the size (that is, the proportion of residential numbers) of each COC. If a stratified sample proportionate to size were to be utilized given this information, we would have to assume that the distribution of nonpublished numbers would not be disproportionate to that of unlisted numbers. Otherwise, mistakes in the calculation of size could produce sample bias by the over- or underrepresentation of some COCs.

(2) Consult the directory for the number of three-digit prefixes in use in the area of concern.

(3) Eliminate those COCs that serve businesses only.

(4) List the banks in use, by prefix:

739 COC	*452 COC*
739 – 1	– 0
– 2	– 1
– 3	– 2
	– 3
	– 4
	– 5
	– 6

Within the 739 COC, no numbers are assigned between 4000 and 9999, and in the 452 COC, no numbers are assigned between 7000 and 9999. To make calls using a four-digit group in those ranges would obviously result in a wasted call to a nonworking number. Using this method, Cooper (1964: 46) generated 57 prefixes and 472 number-blocks of four digits for the Cincinnati area. Naturally, these values will vary by virtue of the geographical scope of the survey.

(5) Create a phone number by adding three random digits to the selected number block. Repeat this procedure until the sample size is reached.

This method does improve the efficiency of calling, since a good portion of the nonworking numbers are not included. Nonpublished numbers have virtually the same probability of selection. This technique represents an improvement over add-a-digit designs, which limit the prospect of selecting those numbers that are spinoffs of listed numbers. By noting any pattern of assigning numbers to commercial enterprises, this method reduces the potential number of wasted calls. The major problem lies with the use of a criss-cross directory that may not always be available or up to date. New banks of 1000 numbers added since the publication of the directory have no chance for inclusion in the sample. As O'Neil (1979) noted, this enhances the bias against rapidly growing areas. In addition, for large surveys a considerable amount of administrative work is required to enumerate the number blocks and assign the random numbers. Hence, this technique is most usable for smaller, local telephone surveys.

RANDOM DIGIT DIALING WITH AID OF TELEPHONE DIRECTORY—SUDMAN METHOD

Since most sources of telephone numbers other than the telephone directory are even more unreliable than this listing, several techniques of sampling that combine random digit dialing with telephone directory information have been proposed. Sudman (1966) and Hauck and Cox (1974) suggest an approach that uses the telephone directory but corrects for the unequal selection probabilities of the other directory-based techniques. The procedure is as follows:

(1) Implement a systematic or random selection of numbers from the appropriate telephone directories.

(2) Discard the last two or three digits of the selected numbers. The remaining digits include the COC, plus the hundreds and the thousands digit (for example, 739-34 or 739-3).

(3) The dropped digits are replaced by two or three randomly selected digits within the range of 00-99 or 000-999. These digits are connected to the 4-5-digit number to create a new seven-digit number. Continue this process until random

numbers are assigned to all previously selected directory numbers and a "specified number of households with *listed* numbers
has been reached" (Frankel and Frankel, 1977: 290).

The first-stage probability of selection is proportional to the
number of unlisted numbers in the directory within a certain
bank. That is, if 10 percent of the listed numbers are within the
739-4 bank, that probability of selection should be reflected in
the sample. The probability of selecting a given number within
the bank is inversely proportional to the number of listed
numbers in it. This is why calls are made until a specific number
of listings have been reached. In addition, efficiency is improved
because banks with a bulk of commercial numbers are less likely
to be included, since commercial numbers will not be selected
from the directory.

Since this technique does rely on telephone directories, there
is the possibility that some listings are out of date and that new
banks will not be included. Thus, as with Cooper's method, this
technique is biased against movers or recent arrivals. The technique also requires considerable clerical work in enumerating
the sample, as well as interviewing time in ascertaining whether
each number called is listed or not. This tends to increase the
probability of nonrandom error (O'Neil, 1979). The administrative overload is a crucial consideration, particularly with
national samples where a considerable number of directories are
involved, but the request for a listing status would only increase
the possibility of refusal. Thus, the marginal cost for replacement is much greater for this method than for other dialing
techniques. Finally, the assignment of a required number of
listed completions per exchange is often based on inadequate
information or cluster size (COC-listed proportion) and could
produce a bias through over- or underrepresenting a prefix.

WAKSBERG DESIGN

Waksberg (1978) has suggested a two-stage cluster design that
has gained considerable popularity with telephone surveys

because it reduces even further the number of unproductive dialings. The Waksberg procedure is as follows:

Stage 1

(1) Implement a random or systematic selection of area code-Central Office Code (AC-COC) combinations. These are obtainable from an AT&T *Long Line Directory.*

(2) Add two random digits to each AC-COC combination.

(3) Prepare a list of all possible eight-digit numbers. These numbers become the Primary Sampling Unit (PSU). If the sample is local, then five-digit combinations result (for example, 539-20–). These combinations provide clusters of 100 numbers each:

AC + COC + hundred, or

(702) + 739 + "2600-2699."

(4) Assign two more random digit numbers to the eight- or five-digit number:

AC + COC + hundred + 2 random numbers, or

(702) + 739 + 26 + 24.

(5) Dial the number: (702) 739-2624.

(6) If the number is a working household number, complete the interview. The PSU of 100 numbers (702-739-26) is retained for additional calls, and those PSUs where the number called is not a residential working number are eliminated from further sampling consideration.

Stage 2

(7) Additional ending digits are selected randomly and dialed within each eight- or five-digit PSU cluster until a certain number of residential listings are reached.

(8) Continue until sample size is reached.

This technique does require a considerable amount of clerical work, particularly in the earlier stages (Waksberg, 1978: 41). However, the first stage need not be duplicated in subsequent studies. The probability of first-stage selection is proportional to the number of working household numbers within a bank, and not to listed numbers, as in the Sudman technique. Thus, the number of completions desired is proportionate to the working numbers within the bank, and not to the listed numbers. The result is a sample selection procedure with probability proportionate to size (PPS).

Each of the random digit dialing methods varies on a number of dimensions including: efficiency, the ability to eliminate nonworking numbers, the amount of clerical work required, and the degree of sample supervision required. O'Neil (1979) provides a comparison, as shown in Table 3.1.

Most of these methods improve efficiency (rate of wasted calls) over the simple random digit dialing design. Cooper (1964) showed an increase of 8 percent efficiency when compared to simple random digit dialing. Hauck and Cox (1974) obtained a .73 efficiency level using the Sudman technique, and Groves and Kahn (1979) obtained an efficiency level of .66 in the second stage of Waksberg, while the first-stage efficiency was .24—virtually no better than the simple random digit dialing design that they also implemented.

Finally, these techniques can be compared in what is known as "design effect"—the difference in precision or sampling error that one would attain using simple random sampling, compared with that attained using the sampling design in question (Groves and Kahn, 1979; O'Neil, 1979). The sample size required under the simple random sampling procedure is what is known as "effective sample size." The value of the design effects, or DEFTs, would equal one if the standard error of the utilized sampling technique were equal to that which would have been attained in a simple random sample of the same magnitude. Thus, high DEFTs are undesirable. While not much comparative information exists, O'Neil (1979) does show that when stratified sampling is implemented in each of the above designs, the DEFTs decrease, though they increase with clustering versions (for example, Waksberg, Stage 1).

TABLE 3.1 Selected Characteristics of Various Random Digit Dialing Designs

Design	Derivation	Elimination of Nonworking Banks	Directories Necessary	Directories Available	Clerical Work Required	Iterative
Simple RDD: append four RDs to known COCs	COC-RRRR	No	No	N/A	None	No
Copper (1964): append three RDs to known COCs + banks	COC-BRRR	Yes	Yes (Criss-cross)	Sometimes (large SMSAs)	Varies (by # of COCs in area sampled)	No
Sudman (1973): directory sampling, replace three RDs	COC-B*RRR	Yes	Yes (regular)	Always	Substantial	Yes
Waksberg (1978): two-stage stratified clustered PPS	AC-COC-RR## replace ## with RR if primary selection is residential	Yes	No	N/A	Moderate	Yes

AC = area code
COC = central office code
B   = known working bank
B* = working bank identified by directory
R   = random digit
= primary number

Source: O'Neil (1979)

Sampling Within Households

Once the sample of households has been drawn, the researcher is faced with the decision of whom to select as a respondent from each selected household. There is no need to implement a selection procedure if the respondent desired has unique characteristics such as male head of household, anyone over age of 60, female full-time worker, or whoever does the shopping. In these cases, it is simply necessary to open the interview with a screen question that asks for this particular person. However, further screening using a variation of one of the selection procedures reported below is necessary if more than one person in the household is a qualified respondent. It is also not necessary to sample within a household if the household itself is the unit of analysis and any adult member can provide the necessary information. Very often, studies on subjects such as consumer behavior, recreation utilization, or child-rearing patterns can solicit information from any adult member of a household.

If a household contains more than one member of the target population, it can be regarded as a cluster of sampling units, and an additional selection procedure must then be implemented. This is particularly true for general population surveys where the only qualification for participation is to be an adult over the age of 18. In these cases, if a selection procedure is not used, it is possible that the resulting sample will be one based on convenience rather than random selection, since interviews will be conducted only with those who happen to be available at the time of the call. There are several strategies of household member selection which have been used by telephone researchers.

The selection procedure suggested by Kish (1949, 1965) requires that at the time of contact with a household the interviewer list each adult separately on a cover sheet form; each is identified by his or her relationship to the head of the household, by sex, and by age (Kish, 1965: 398). It is then necessary for the interviewer to assign a serial number for each

TABLE 3.2   Summary of Eight Categories Used for Selecting One Adult in Each Dwelling

Category Number	1	2	3	4	5	6 or more
			Number of Adults in Household			
			Select Adult Numbered:			
A	1	1	1	1	1	1
B1	1	1	1	1	2	2
B2	1	1	1	2	2	2
C	1	1	2	2	3	3
D	1	2	2	3	4	4
E1	1	2	3	3	3	5
E2	1	2	3	4	5	5
F	1	2	3	4	5	6

Source: Kish (1965: 399)

adult (1, 2, 3, and so forth) by decreasing age, beginning with the oldest male and counting all males first, then repeating the procedure beginning with the oldest female. The interviewer then consults one of eight categories (Table 3.2) to determine the specific adult to be interviewed. This selection varies with the number of adults in the household. The assignment of categories to households or numbers can be made in advance of actual contact. If this is not possible, the interviewer must match households and categories using a sequence assigned by the field director. While this technique provides for an equi-probability selection of respondents, there are some practical problems associated with its use.

In the first place, it is quite time consuming to ask for this information prior to initiating the interview. This may not be a significant problem in a household survey where the physical presence of the interviewer in the home of the respondent sets up a demand situation in which the respondent feels compelled to provide such information. However, it is important in the telephone situation to preserve as much time as possible for the actual questioning, since there is some resistance to lengthy telephone interviews. In addition, asking for this information, which is personal in nature, before providing much detail on the nature of the study can result in the respondent becoming suspicious of the purpose of the call and hanging up. Finally, the Kish technique puts a significant burden on the interviewer by requiring him or her to record the household information, assign a number to each adult, and then decide on the appropriate respondent. The potential for sampling error is thereby enhanced. This technique is probably more suited to face-to-face surveys then to research by telephone.

One adaptation of the Kish format to telephone surveys was made by Troldahl and Carter (1964), who sought to reduce the time consumed in the determination of the appropriate respondent and to decrease the possibility of a termination of the interview in its introductory phase as a result of the respondent being unsure of the call's purpose. The authors admit to a bias against the selection of the middle-aged adult in a household of three adults of the same sex, but since this is an infrequent occurrence, the bias is not viewed as serious.

Figure 3.1 and Table 3.3 report the procedure used by Troldahl and Carter for selecting respondents for interviews. After a brief introduction, the interviewer begins by asking two questions:

(1) Including yourself, how many persons 18 years or older live in your household?
(2) How many of them are men?

The interviewer then follows an explicit procedure (Figure 3.1) for selecting the respondent wherein four categories are randomly assigned to household numbers. Troldahl and Carter reported good results with this technique but did not significantly reduce refusals when compared to the Kish strategy.

Bryant (1975) varied this technique because it was discovered that the Troldahl-Carter method selected a disproportionate number of females, particularly from smaller households. Her adaptation was to drop one of the four categories every second

Q-1 The first one is, how many people 18 years and older live in this household, including yourself? _____

CIRCLE ANSWER IN THIS ROW

Q-2 How many of them are men?

		1	2	3	4
	0	WOMAN	OLDEST WOMAN	YOUNGEST WOMAN	YOUNGEST WOMAN
CIRCLE ANSWER IN THIS COLUMN	1	MAN	MAN	MAN	OLDEST WOMAN
	2		OLDEST MAN	YOUNGEST MAN	YOUNGEST MAN
	3			YOUNGEST MAN	OLDEST MAN
	4				OLDEST MAN

(INTERVIEWER: CIRCLE CATEGORY AT INTERSECTION AND USE IN THIS SENTENCE)

Okay, according to the method used by our university, I need to interview the

_____in your household.

        (age -sex)

(IF PERSON ON LINE IS *RIGHT* SEX)   (IF PERSON ON LINE IS *WRONG* SEX)

Would that be you?

          YES 1
          No 2

                          May I speak with that person?

                                  YES 1

WHEN SELECTED PERSON   No 2
ANSWERS, REPEAT INTRO-
DUCTION AND START   When may I call back to reach
INTERVIEW   (him/her)?

                                So that I will know who to ask for
                                what is (his/her) name? (REPEAT
                                BACK TO BE SURE YOU HAVE IT
                                AND SHOW PRONUNCIATION IF
                                IT IS A PROBLEM). "We only need the
                                the person's first name, the last name
(START INTERVIEW)   isn't necessary."

Source: Troldahl and Carter (1964). Reprinted by permission of the American Marketing Association.

FIGURE 3.1   Procedure for Selecting Respondents

TABLE 3.3   Categories Used For Selecting Respondents

Total Number of Men in Household	Total Number of Adults in Household			
	1	2	3	4
Version I				
0	Woman	Oldest Woman	Youngest Woman	Youngest Woman
1	Man	Man	Man	Oldest Woman
2		Oldest Man	Youngest Man	Youngest Man
3			Youngest Man	Oldest Man
4+				Oldest Man
Version II				
0	Woman	Youngest Woman	Youngest Woman	Oldest Woman
1	Man	Man	Oldest Woman	Man
2		Oldest Man	Woman	Oldest Woman
3			Youngest Man	Woman or Oldest Woman
4+				Oldest Man
Version III				
0	Woman	Youngest Woman	Oldest Woman	Oldest Woman
1	Man	Woman	Man	Youngest Woman
2		Youngest Man	Oldest Man	Oldest Man
3			Oldest Man	Youngest Man
4+				Youngest Man
Version IV				
0	Woman	Oldest Woman	Oldest Woman	Youngest Woman
1	Man	Woman	Youngest Woman	Man
2		Youngest Man	Woman	Youngest Woman
3			Oldest Man	Woman or Youngest Woman
4+				Youngest Man

Source: Troldahl and Carter (1964) "Random selection of respondents within households in phone surveys." Reprinted by permission of the American Marketing Association.

time it appeared in the rotation. As such, the assignment sequence would be:

Versions Assigned

	I	II	III	IV
Time 1	I	II	III	IV
Time 2	–	II	III	IV
Time 3	I	–	III	IV
Time 4	I	II	III	–
Time 5	I	II	III	IV
Time 6	–	II	III	IV

Using the same question sequence as Troldahl and Carter (1964), Groves and Kahn (1979) asked for the number of females instead of males. They found no difference in response rates between the telephone and face-to-face samples using this respondent selection technique.

Questioning the value of asking any household composition questions at all (because of the refusal problems), Hagen and Collier (1982) compared the Troldahl-Carter technique with an alternative procedure that eliminated all household composition techniques. Respondent selection forms were printed with the designated respondent predetermined to be one of four possibilities: oldest man, youngest man, oldest woman, or youngest woman (Hagen and Collier, 1982: 3). After a brief introduction, interviewers simply asked for the designated respondent. One-half of the national sample of 2500 households received each treatment. Their results showed fewer referrals produced by the alternative approach, and demographic differences between the two groups were not significant. The authors also concluded that their procedure reduced respondent burden and decreased interviewing costs.

Respondent selection within households is necessary to translate a sample of households into a sample of the target population. The implementation of any of the above techniques is not

without problems, however. First, interviewers must be adequately trained and supervised on its implementation. This part
of an interview is difficult to administer and calls for skill in
decision making on the part of the interviewer. Since this is part
of the initial phase of the interview, the respondent is likely to
ask questions with regard to the study, including why the
interviewer needs household composition information. The
interviewer will have to be resourceful without providing
answers that might bias any subsequent responses. Not all
interviewers have this capability, even after extensive training.
Second, female respondents will often resist a procedure that
asks for males, particularly when there are none present in the
household. Since more and more households are headed by
single females, this resistance is bound to increase. The potential
for resistance as the result of inquiries into household composition is one reason that it is very important to be able to create
an initial positive rapport or sense of legitimacy with a respondent during the introduction to the survey; a high rate of refusal
will be the result if this effort is not made.

Drawing a representative sample is not as serious a problem
for telephone surveys as it has been in the past. It is now
possible, by using a combination of techniques, to draw a
sample that will include all of the relevant characteristics of a
population in their existing proportions. There are, however,
some sampling-related problems that require further attention,
such as obtaining up-to-date information from the telephone
companies, converting refusals, reducing substitutions, and dealing with those who do not have a phone.

Still, these problems are no excuse for not paying considerable attention to respondent selection procedures. The perceived quality of telephone survey research may often rest, with
clients and the general public, on the ability to obtain truly
representative views and opinions. As valuable as the information provided by the survey is, its import can be severely
compromised if the sampling procedures are judged inadequate
or the sampling error excessive. Any difficulties associated with

sampling should be acknowledged in the early phases of a project to head off any misunderstandings or conflicts that may occur later.

All sampling decisions are, of course, contingent on research goals, population characteristics, and available resources. Every researcher wants to implement the purest, most error-free design, but very often the practical nature of such problems as population accessibility, funding, potential respondent burden, and the like force decisions to compromise scientific standards as the result of the exigencies of survey research.

Notes

1. Occasionally, it is possible to obtain a list of prefixes in use from a computer tape available from the local telephone company. Access to this source varies with the degree of cooperation provided by the company.

2. Area codes follow state lines or recognizable physical geographic features (for example, rivers, highways, or lakes). These are drawn to minimize the splitting of communities of interest or recognized metropolitan areas. Approximately 150 area code designations are available from AT&T: 130 of these are currently in use.

3. The only recognizable pattern to the assignment of numbers to the 1000 series is the designation of 9000 to pay phones or coin exchanges. This should be noted in sample selection.

CHAPTER 4

QUESTIONNAIRE DESIGN

Before the sampling procedures have been decided on, we must begin to consider how best to frame the questions in order to obtain a completed interview. That is, once a respondent has been selected, we want to motivate that person to make two decisions favorable to the survey. The first is to commit to participate. Sometime shortly after the interviewer makes the first contact, the prospective respondent will probably say something to himself like: "Survey of my community, sounds interesting. Okay," or "Not another poll, forget it!" As will be pointed out below, obtaining a favorable decision on participation is largely dependent on the nature of the introduction to the survey. The second decision made by the respondent, once he or she has committed to participate, concerns the quality of that participation. In this case, the respondent decides to participate in a truthful manner, giving replies that reflect actual feelings, knowledge, and behavior rather than responses that represent a desire to please the interviewer, are deliberately distorted, or consist of artificial reactions to the way a question is worded or phrased by the interviewer. Response quality depends on the trust the respondent feels for the survey, the topic, and the interviewer, and on the manner in which questions are worded and arranged.

This chapter will look at the relation of questionnaire construction and question wording in telephone surveys to the potential for response effects or nonsampling error.[1] Chapter 5 will discuss the effect of interviewers on response patterns, in addition to other administrative considerations. I will offer several suggestions on construction and wording, but the reader should bear in mind that although these suggestions are based on experience and sound principle, they may not strictly apply to his or her research situation. Variations in questionnaire construction and question wording are common given the nature of the research problem and the population being surveyed. There are a multitude of sources for the general principles of questionnaire design and question wording (Payne, 1951; Babbie, 1979; Bradburn and Sudman, 1979; Backstrom and Hursh-Cesar, 1981), and I do not intend to repeat them here. However, since most of these guidelines are written for face-to-face surveys, it will be necessary to demonstrate how these maxims can be applied to telephone surveys. In most cases, however, questionnaire construction principles formulated for face-to-face surveys are also applicable to telephone surveys.

Since telephone interviews depend solely on verbal communication, there are some aspects of the face-to-face situation that cannot be duplicated in a telephone interview. First, visual aids, such as response cards or diagrams, cannot be used to aid the respondent. Nor can the interviewer depend on visual cues from respondents that might reveal a misunderstanding of the question or boredom with the interview. In addition, the interviewer is not able to observe the physical surroundings of the respondent for additional data or validation evidence. Finally, in a telephone interview the respondent has no chance to "size up" or make judgments regarding the personal characteristics of the interviewer, other than voice quality, in advance of participating. Each of these interviewer characteristics can have an impact on whether or not an agreement to participate is obtained from the respondent.

The telephone questionnaire can never be a duplicate of the mail survey instrument, either. In this case, the presence of the interviewer as an intermediary reduces the necessity of depending exclusively on questionnaire format and appearance to stimulate a response. Just as the telephone survey is totally dependent on a single means of communication—oral—so is the mail survey totally dependent on a single form of communication—

the written word.[2] By emphasizing certain aspects of the research purpose in the introduction, the telephone interviewer must persuade the prospective respondent to complete the interview, usually without the help of any previous communication or the possibility of the respondent anticipating the nature of the survey by being able to see the questionnaire in advance. This is particularly true with random digit dialing, where a respondent and interviewer know nothing about each other prior to opening a conversation. In a mail survey, respondents can obtain some idea of the nature of the survey by reviewing the mailing envelope, the questionnaire cover sheet, and other related materials prior to responding. Thus, because of the total dependence on oral communication, special attention must be paid to designing a telephone questionnaire that will assist the interviewer as much as possible in retaining the attention of the respondent from start to finish.

In the case of the telephone questionnaire, design and construction are based on utility rather than aesthetics. While it does not have to look pretty, the telephone questionnaire format must be designed in such a manner that it can be easily administered by the interviewer, followed by the respondent, and coded by the data processor. The interviewer's job is made more difficult if instructions are unclear; if response categories are not clearly differentiated from questions; if the question wording does not permit a conversational tone; if the question order does not "flow" with the aid of transitional statements, adequate question introductions, or clearly marked branching sequences on screen or filter questions; if question placement is irregular, without apparent topical organization; and/or if it is necessary to turn pages frequently. Interviewer error, in the form of improper question reading or inaccurate recording of responses, is reduced and productivity enhanced if a smooth questionnaire format is provided (Labaw, 1980).

Since the respondent is totally dependent on the interviewer to communicate the intent of the questionnaire verbally, format or design is especially important in order to maintain the respondent's attention. The task of responding to a telephone survey is already made difficult by the demand for a high level of concentration (Dillman, 1978). This situation does not need to be exacerbated by irregular question order, unclear instructions on the desired response pattern, or delays in the reinforcement of responses because the interviewer is searching for a response category. In addition, a lack of transitional statements informing the respondent of a topic shift or a change in the level of question complexity, the demands of an uncomfortable "pace," and/or a lack of clarity in wording all can make responding more difficult. Furthermore, if the respondent resents being called to the phone unexpectedly and the initial anxiety of responding to a stranger over the phone has not been overcome via the introductory message, there is a good chance of getting distorted responses or even a refusal to participate if the questionnaire flow presents any of the problems mentioned above. Finally, if the respondent's attention is not riveted to the task at hand—listening and responding to survey questions—response error is more likely due to the distractions of a television program, conversations of family members, or other factors of the social context of the interview.

Finally, before any questionnaire is implemented, it should be reviewed by a data processing analyst or coder. Very often the coder can provide insight into the arrangement of response categories and even the types of responses that can be anticipated. Precoding is usually done on telephone questionnaires in order to save time and energy by avoiding the use of individual code sheets. From a formatting standpoint, however, coding devices have to be clearly differentiated in order to prevent confusion on the part of the interviewer. In other words, the codes (for example, column numbers) should not get in the way of the smooth administration of the questionnaire.

The questionnaire is a totality, a whole, or as some have said, a "gestalt" (Labaw, 1980) that is greater than the sum of its parts. Each part is related to every other part, and all are organically tied together by a web of transitions under the umbrella of the research problem. In one sense, achieving this balance or interdependence is an art rather than a hard science.

All components must be treated with careful attention, and all must be coordinated to achieve high-quality responses. The work of weaving the questionnaire together begins with the introductory statement.

Introducing the Questionnaire

Except for research reported by Dillman et al. (1976) and brief discussions by Dillman (1978) and Groves and Kahn (1979), the literature on telephone surveys is not very helpful in providing guidelines for constructing an introductory message that will be likely to produce a favorable decision to participate. This is somewhat surprising, since it is a well-documented fact that most terminations or refusals take place after the introduction but before the first question. Thus, a respondent will usually give the interviewer a chance to state the details of the survey before deciding not to participate. Given this response pattern, constructing an introductory message should command the same (or even more) attention as question design and arrangement.

The introductory message must accomplish for the telephone interview what the physical presence of an interviewer, in combination with a standardized introduction, does for the face-to-face survey, and what packaging and cover letters do for mail surveys (Dillman, 1978). In the case of face-to-face interviews and mail surveys, respondents have time to observe and listen to an interviewer or to evaluate the mailed materials thoroughly (including the opportunity to assess the length of the questionnaire) before making a decision to participate. The unanticipated phone call and the almost immediate request for consent to an interview give the respondent little time to evaluate what he or she should do. It is likely that a good many refusals can be attributed to the frustration a respondent may feel when faced with a decision based on little or no information. In fact, the respondent may not even "hear" the bulk of the introductory message because he or she is so busy concentrating on whether or not to participate. Perhaps it would be preferable to delay the request for an interview as long as possible in favor of providing a thorough description of the nature of the survey, the sponsor, and the role of the respondent before asking for an interview.

Building respondent trust and overcoming the initial reluctance to participate in a survey begins with the introductory message which, at the minimum, identifies the caller, explains why the call is being made, what kind of information is requested, the conditions (that is, degree of confidentiality) under which the interview will be conducted, and the benefits of participation.

PRE-INTERVIEW CONTACT

While the available research shows that variations in conditions (such as offering a reward in the form of a copy of the results, or emphasizing the social utility of the research) produce no differences in response rates (Dillman et al., 1976), it remains the responsibility of the researcher to write an introduction that is informative and persuasive and that in no way compromises the identity of the respondent. Where a list is available, it is possible to reduce the problem of resistance by means of a precontact memo informing the prospective respondent about the nature of the survey and the approximate time to expect a call requesting the interview.

The Preletter. Preletters have been shown to depress refusal rates and improve data quality for general public surveys (Dillman et al., 1976). Not only does such a letter provide information about a survey, but it reduces the element of surprise that is associated with an unanticipated phone call, thus giving the respondent time to consider the benefits and costs of his or her participation. The preletter also provides a symbolic representation of the authenticity of the survey in case respondents might be concerned that mention of a survey was merely a smoke-screen for a sales pitch. It has also been discovered that respon-

UNIVERSITY OF NEVADA, LAS VEGAS

4505 Maryland Parkway   Las Vegas, Nevada 89154

Research Facility and
Telephone Survey Center
702-739-3322

College of Arts & Letters

November 1, 1981

Mr. John C. Jones
4505 Maryland Parkway
Las Vegas, NV 89154

Dear Mr. Jones:

During the week of November 14-20 one of our interviewers
will be calling your home in connection with a survey of
Southern Nevada residents on their views about the most important
issues facing their community.

Your name and number were selected at random from the local
telephone directory. We are writing this letter because some
persons prefer being informed in advance about a request for an
interview. When our interviewer calls he or she will request to
speak to an adult, either you or another member of your household.
This is done to be sure all Clark County opinions are represented
in the survey.

The interview should only last about ten minutes. Naturally,
all of your responses, or those of another member of your household, will be confidential, and your participation is strictly voluntary.

Your participation will be greatly appreciated since this is
a very important study. If you have any questions, please call
me at 739-3320.

Sincerely,

James H. Frey
Project Director

FIGURE 4.1

dents seem more cooperative and that interviews are easier to
begin when an advance letter has been mailed (Dillman et al.,
1976).

The letter need not be lengthy; it should never be over one
page (see Figure 4.1). It should be printed on letterhead stationery, with a personal salutation and individually signed in blue
ink. The contents of the letter should include an introductory
statement informing the respondent that he or she will be called
and the approximate time of the call, as well as some indication
of how the respondent was selected (for example, random
procedure using phone book or list of organization members). It

is at this point that the recipient of the letter is informed that someone else in the household may be selected for participation. This must be noted, particularly if a procedure to sample members of the household is to be implemented. In addition, the preletter should contain a description of the research problem. In this case, the description must provide sufficient information to arouse the interest of the respondent, but at the same time avoid making the research goal seem so complex that the respondent may decide that he or she is not qualified to participate. The terms used should follow the maxims for question wording, such as avoiding inflammatory terms or "leading" phrases. Of course, the description should not project false images by purporting to study one topic and then be followed by questions about another. There should also be a guarantee of confidentiality, a statement of the approximate length of the interview, and an expression of appreciation for considering the interview. One should be honest about the length of time the interview will take, and if calling long distance, inform the respondent of that fact, since this could easily enhance the importance of the study in his or her eyes and aid in obtaining a positive response.

Pre-Interview Telephone Contact. A preliminary phone call can also be made for the purpose of introduction. These calls are made to sample households not to request information, but to inform respondents of their selection for the survey and of how the selection was made. The precall introduces the interviewer to the household, and the respondent is told at that time that a second call will be coming. This works to establish trust and increases the probability of a favorable response to a second call, provided that no adverse effects occur after the first call (Reingen and Kernan, 1977). Groves and MagiLavy (1981) tested these notions using a dual-call procedure in a national survey.

Using the framework provided by what is called the "foot-in-the-door" technique, often implemented by marketing researchers,[3] Groves and MagiLavy (1981) implemented the Waksberg sampling procedure and on the first call asked respondents to answer just two questions on health and then verified the phone number. They also asked for the name of the person with whom they spoke in order to have a reference for the second call. The second call then requested compliance with a 30-minute interview. To test the effect of this "foot-in-the-door" procedure, an equivalent sample received only the single request for a 30-minute interview. Surprisingly, the overall response rates (80 and 81 percent, respectively) were not significantly different. Hence, the authors concluded that call-backs and refusal conversion procedures are just as effective in producing desired response rates and also less costly than the two-call procedure. The "foot-in-the-door" technique does have possibilities for survey research, but further investigation on just how and with what populations this technique is most effective is needed.

NO PRECONTACT

Most telephone surveys today utilize random digit dialing, which does not depend on a list of names and therefore makes the use of a preletter impossible. Precalls are not ruled out by random digit dialing, however, as demonstrated by the work of Groves and MagiLavy (1981). However, their inability to generate significant differences when compared to the results of not using a precontact suggests that precalls do not necessarily improve response rates or data quality for random digit surveys. Even when lists are available, it is rare, because of considerations of cost and time, for a preletter or precall to be utilized. Thus, most prospective respondents are called "cold turkey" and asked to complete an interview over the phone. The introduction is then varied, depending on whether the sampling frame was an available directory or simply random numbers, with no additional information about the respondent beyond the selected number. Figure 4.2 illustrates the introduction used with directory sampling, and Figure 4.3 contains an introduction for a random digit dialing survey.

Hello. Is this the _____ residence?

    (If Wrong Number: Terminate the call with something like
    "SORRY TO HAVE BOTHERED YOU.")

This is _____ calling from the Telephone Survey
Center at the University of Nevada, Las Vagas. We are conducting a survey of
Southern Nevada residents about their views of the most important issues facing their
community.

    If a prior letter was sent, insert comment about letter, such as: "Early this month
    a letter describing the survey was sent to your household explaining the study.
    Did you receive it?"

    If Yes: PROCEED WITH REMAINDER OF INTRODUCTION.

    If No: "I am sorry it did not reach you. The letter was to inform you of this call
          and the nature of the study."

          PROCEED WITH INTRODUCTION.

Your number was selected at random from a local telephone directory, and your
responses will be confidential.

INSERT SELECTION PROCEDURES; REPEAT INTRODUCTORY STATEMENT
ABOUT NATURE OF STUDY.

The interview should take approximately ten minutes of your time. Please feel free to
ask questions at any time and you may withhold your response to any item if you
wish. Okay?

FIGURE 4.2   Introduction With Directory Sampling

It is in the situation of random dialing that the introductory
statement of the telephone interview is most crucial. In order to
enhance the credibility of the study, the interviewer should first
state his or her complete name. A call from "Mary" or "Jack" is
suggestive of something suspicious to the respondent, particu-
arly if the person calling is not willing to give a complete name.
The source of the phone call (for example, the University of
Nevada, Las Vegas) is the next bit of information provided. The
interviewer should be prepared to respond to a question such
as: "Just what is Behavioral Dynamics and Surveys?" regarding
the study sponsor. In fact, it is good practice to have trained
interviewers to deal with a variety of questions on the nature of
the survey, the profile of the study sponsor, the manner of
selection, and so forth. Very often these questions will arise

Hello. Is this _____?
                     (Number)

If No: STATE YOU HAVE REACHED A WRONG NUMBER AND TERMI-
         NATE THE INTERVIEW. ALSO TERMINATE IF A NONRESIDEN-
         TIAL NUMBER.

If Yes: PROCEED.

This is _____ calling from the Telephone Survey
           (Interviewer's full name)
Center of the University of Nevada, Las Vegas. We are conducting a survey of
Southern Nevada residents about their views of the most important issues facing their
community.

INSERT SELECTION OR SCREEN PROCEDURE.

REPEAT ABOVE.

Your number was selected at random and your responses will be confidential. The
interview should take approximately ten minutes. Feel free to ask questions at any
time, and you may withhold a response to any item if you wish. Okay?

**FIGURE 4.3   Introduction With Random Dialing—No Pre-Interview
                Contact**

during the introduction, and the response given must be judged
satisfactory or else a refusal could result. To assist the interviewer, a list of anticipated questions and acceptable answers
should be provided (see Chapter 5).

The message continues with statements on how the respondent was selected, the nature of the topic, how confidentiality
will be ensured, and on the approximate length of the interview.
The final "Okay?" alludes to requesting an affirmative decision
of the respondent, and a pause before asking the first question
satisfies the requirement of informed consent, in that the
respondent has the opportunity to refuse after hearing what the
study is about and being given the chance to ask questions. This
request to go ahead also satisfies the condition that participation in the interview be voluntary. Some researchers utilize an
alternative approach in which the statements of confidentiality
and voluntary participation are included as lead-ins to the first
question. For example, the interviewer might begin with the

following: "Our first question concerns your feelings on certain political issues. Keep in mind that your answers are confidential and that you may feel free not to respond to any question." I prefer to include this statement in the introduction and to remind the respondent of the confidential nature of his or her answers later in the interview.

A final function of the introductory message is to screen to the relevant population or household member. Standard household member selection procedures can be administered as recommended in Chapter 3. However, sometimes a household will not contain an eligible person for the survey, or the household itself is not eligible. For example, most political polls seek responses only from registered voters. Therefore, it is necessary to screen for an eligible respondent (that is, a voter) early in the introduction but not before the purpose of the survey has been given.

HOW MUCH INFORMATION

There is some debate about how much information to give a study prior to asking the questions. The traditional view holds that as little as possible should be disclosed to avoid bias and preconceived answers. The true purpose of the study will be revealed in the nature of the questions asked or in a post-interview debriefing (Parten, 1950). This view is giving way to a position which holds that respondents should be given considerable information. This is a matter of treating respondents with respect and also guards against any accusations of malpractice or unethical conduct. While more experimentation is necessary, some research (for example, Sobal, 1978) indicates that no relation between the amount of information given in the introductory message and the rate of completions. Additional work will have to be done to show the true relation between data quality and the amount of information provided to the respondent. Meanwhile, individual researchers will have to decide on the amount of information to be provided. The extent to which study purposes are revealed depends on the complexity of the

TABLE 4.1   Items for Inclusion in Introductory Message

Mandatory

(1) Who is calling—interviewer's full name
(2) Identify research organization or sponsor of the research
(3) Study topic—nature or purpose of the research
(4) Selection procedure
(5) Protection of respondent—confidentiality
(6) Approximate length of interview
(7) Opportunity to refuse—informed consent and volunteer participation
(8) Opportunity to ask questions

Optional

(1) Offer of incentive
(2) Future use—how results will be used
(3) Format—style of interview—open or closed items
(4) Sponsor—who hired the research organization
(5) Any unusual expectations of the respondent—"recall to childhood"
(6) Detailed discussion of research purpose

research topic, the characteristics of the respondent (for example, education), and the length of the interview (the longer the interview, the more time taken in the introduction). Table 4.1 lists the items that must be covered in an introduction, along with some optional items.

One final point with respect to the introduction and first questions: Just as jargon, inflammatory terms, and "leading" phrases should not be used within questions, they should not be utilized in introductory statements, either. The introduction should be neutral in tone so that researcher expectancy factors are not conveyed to the respondent. For example, the introduction to a 1981 quality-of-life survey by the Nevada Survey Center deliberately omitted any mention of the MX missile in order to avoid the possibility of respondents feeling that the study, originating in an academic institution, was looking for an unfavorable interpretation of the impact of the MX. In addition, if the term "MX Missile" had been used in the introduction to the questionnaire, respondents might have used the MX as a referent in their responses to all of the community quality-of-life terms, since the MX controversy was quite prominent and visible at the time of this survey. We wanted respondents' perceptions of the quality of life before the implementation of the MX, and then we asked them to assess the probable impact of the MX installation in Nevada on each quality-of-life item. It is likely that the differences in response would have been less meaningful if the MX had been a referent for both response series. This pattern of response was verified in our pretesting which, of course, is crucial to the development of any phase of a questionnaire.

This point also illustrates the "whole" character of the questionnaire. The introduction is tied to the first items; the later material is related to subsequent questions, and all is related to the research topic. This emphasis continues with the grouping of questions.

Question Order[4]

The arrangement of questions should take into account the expectations and tasks of the interviewer, respondent, and coder. For each, the questions are part of a whole, not isolated or separate from other items. Each question is part of a context of other questions, as well as part of a continuous flow of questions. The researcher needs to be very conscious of the fact that question order can have an effect on the manner in which a question is asked and on its response. Both could result in response error beyond acceptable limits.

The interviewer's questions should flow in a clear and orderly fashion. Instructions—such as those used with screen or filter questions and with guides to recording responses—should be clearly distinguished from questions. Question order contributes greatly to the ability of the interviewer to maintain a conversational tone while administering the questionnaire by following clearly defined instructions. Figure 4.4 illustrates this pattern. The interviewer knows that any information in boxes or in caps is *not* to be read to the respondent. The written instructions, plus the arrows designating question order, reduce interviewer

1. The federal government is considering placing the MX missile in the state of Nevada. Would you favor or oppose that installation?

       1   Opposed

       2   Favor

       3   Don't know (DO NOT READ AND GO TO Q2)

IF "FAVOR" ASK:

       1-A   What do you think will be the major benefit of the MX to Nevada?

               PROBE IF RESPONDENT UNSURE
               PROBE FOR ELABORATION

               IF THE RESPONDENT NAMES MORE THAN ONE, ASK FOR THE *MOST* IMPORTANT BENEFIT

IF "OPPOSE" ASK:

       1-B   What do you think will be the major problem with the MX for Nevada?

               PROBE IF RESPONDENT UNSURE
               PROBE FOR ELABORATION

               IF THE RESPONDENT NAMES MORE THAN ONE, ASK FOR THE *MOST* IMPORTANT PROBLEM

FIGURE 4.4   **Instructions to Interviewer**

confusion and promote conversational continuity during administration of the questionnaire.

Despite the introductory material and the apparent agreement of the respondent to continue, termination could occur if the respondent is confused by the sequence of questions or if the burden of responding is excessive as the result of a haphazard and illogical (at least to the respondent) question sequence. A smooth-flowing question sequence provides a positive context for response; not finding the question order objectionable or excessively difficult, the respondent may feel that participation is worth his or her time and that the research is credible (Dillman, 1978). However, erratic questions or response category sequences increase respondent burden and the potential for subsequent misinterpretations of questions and their meaning. In addition, a burdensome question order increases the potential for a respondent to simply hang up because the questionnaire as presented over the phone appeared disorganized or did not make sense. Thus, a logical and organized question order reduces the potential for error, either as deviation from "true" item responses or in terms of overall response rate. Even after the introduction, the questionnaire must hold the respondent's attention and motivate continued participation.

The work of the coder is facilitated if answer categories and instructions to the interviewer on how to record a response are clearly marked. Predetermined response categories make it easier for the interviewer to code a response while at the same time keeping the interview moving in a purposeful, yet conversational manner. The presence of predetermined response categories makes it easier for the coder to transfer data to a code sheet or keypunch card. If open-ended questions are used, the interviewer's and coder's work can be aided by the existence of a precode of anticipated answers, plus clear instructions on how to code a response to this type of item. A pretest can be of great assistance in uncovering any problems with coding and recording responses, as well as being a source of open-end precode categories.

Response error and even premature termination can result from the mechanical sequencing effects of question grouping or from the arrangement of the first questions. Even more serious is response error due to the influence of preceding questions on responses to a later question. These are called context effects or meaning transfers (Schuman and Presser, 1981). Survey results and response patterns to specific questions must be judged in terms of the context in which questions are asked. Most questionnaires are constructed without concern for order effects, such as the salience of item topic or the relation of a general to a specific question. In fact, until Schuman and Presser published their systematic review of data available on question-order effects, survey researchers had paid little attention to the problem.

This disregard is evident when researchers readily exchange questions or implement questions asked in one survey, often unrelated to the researcher's topic, in another survey. For example, we might use a novel item on political attitudes or a Michigan item on gun control in a survey on attitudes toward crime. Even though we could justify the inclusion of those items, we cannot be sure that a portion of the response is not due to a different context for the questions rather than to a reflection of the "true" attitude. Despite their cautionary warnings, Schuman and Presser (1981: 74) suggest that order effects are difficult to predict, neither pervasive enough to be overwhelming nor sufficiently rare to be of no concern. Their experimental data show that question order effects can be serious and deserve consideration in any survey. This problem will be discussed in greater detail below.

Response error and recording error can be reduced by ordering the questions with the interviewer, respondent, and coder in mind. General principles of question sequencing can be found in selected textbooks on research methodology. However, there are some points that need to be emphasized because of the special nature of the telephone interview. These items are: (1) the importance of the first question, (2) the grouping of questions and response patterns, (3) the use of transitional statements, and (4) question sequencing.

THE FIRST QUESTIONS

Once researchers have obtained a commitment from a person to participate after having delivered the introductory message, many seem to forget that they still have the task of maintaining respondent interest and making response as easy as possible. A lack of attention to these obligations is often demonstrated by the first few questions.

The initial questions should be items directly related to the topic of the interview as expressed in the introductory statement (see Figure 4.5). Even if that statement is effective and the interest of the respondent in the research topic has been

Hello. This is _____ calling from the Telephone
                        (Full name)
Survey Center of the University of Nevada, Las Vegas. We are conducting a survey of
Nevada residents on their opinions and perceptions of the quality of life in the state.
Your number was selected at random by computer. We have just a few questions we
would like to ask. Your answers will be confidential and the interview will only take
about 5 minutes. Feel free to ask questions at any time. Okay?

1. First, I would like to ask how you feel about Nevada as a place to live. Do you
   consider it _____?
                   (READ ALTERNATIVES)

   (1) Very desirable
   (2) Somewhat desirable
   (3) Somewhat undesirable
   (4) Undesirable

   (8) No opinion, DK   DO NOT READ
   (9) Refusal

2. Next, I would like to ask the same question about the community in which
   you live, or live closest to. As a place to live, do you consider your community:
                   (READ ALTERNATIVES)

   (1) Very desirable
   (2) Somewhat desirable
   (3) Somewhat undesirable
   (4) Undesirable

   (8) No opinion, DK   DO NOT READ
   (9) Refusal

FIGURE 4.5   First Questions

stimulated, that interest can be deflated rapidly by an unrelated
first item. For example, the introduction to a survey on political issues and candidate preference may have stimulated a
prospective candidate to be ready to "speak his mind" on these
topics, only to be let down by a first question such as: "What is
your age?" or "Do you approve or disapprove of the new street
lighting system?" A respondent is likely to question the relevance of these items, in addition to feeling that he or she has

been drawn into a commitment to the survey under false pretenses. Some respondents might even go so far as to think that a sales pitch is going to follow, since the first question did not address the stated research interest.

The first questions set the theme for the remainder of the interview. If these flow easily from the introduction, then a sense of order is projected that should be retained throughout the interview. They also establish the "rapport effect," where the respondent begins to feel a sense of trust in the interview situation and a willingness to cooperate to the fullest and most truthful extent. Dillman (1978) suggests that the first question be a closed item relevant to the topic, interesting, and easy to answer. The second question could be open-ended, allowing the respondent to express a view and to find his or her "telephone voice." Instead of opening with two closed items in the MX survey of Figure 4.5, we could have implemented the following sequence of closed- and open-ended items:

1. First, I would like to ask how you feel about Nevada as a state in which you live. Do you consider it:
   (READ ALTERNATIVES)

GO TO 1A —	1. Very desirable
	2. Somewhat desirable
GO TO 1B —	3. Somewhat undesirable
	4. Undesirable
GO TO 2 —	8. No opinion, don't know
	9. Refusal to answer

    1A   What specifically do you find desirable about living in Nevada?

    1B   What specifically do you find undesirable about living in Nevada?

This sequence of questions fulfilled the function of capturing the respondent's interest, on the one hand and, on the other, it prepared the respondent for a series of items related to the quality of life. If we had moved to another topic area, the flow would have been disrupted and the respondent's concentration on quality of life broken. Thus, the introduction and the first few questions are very important as guides into more complicated questions that may require even greater concentration on the part of the respondent.

QUESTION GROUPINGS AND TRANSITIONAL STATEMENTS

It is usually the case that a questionnaire will contain items pertaining to several different, often unrelated topics, or to several subtopics of a larger research problem. In order to facilitate administration of the questionnaire by the interviewer and comprehension by the respondent, two considerations are most important.

First, questions should be grouped according to topic and in a manner that allows the respondent's perception of the relationship between items to prevail. Question relationships, as they are defined by the project director or researcher, may not always match the logic of the relationship or meaning content as perceived by the respondent. For example, the research problem may have something to do with alienation, and the researcher has several different measures to apply in order ultimately to construct an index of alienation. There may be some attitude items, as well as items on association memberships, friendship patterns, and family life, all of which are designed to obtain some measure of alienation. If the questions were grouped according to the variable, their flow would be irregular and appear to be disorganized. Imagine the confusion on the part of the respondent when he or she faces a family life question, followed by an organization membership question, an attitudinal item, and then a question of friendships. This type of pattern will not only fatigue the respondent, it also puts each question into a context that produces undesirable response effects because of the variation in interpretation that is possible as a result of "mixing items." In each case, the respondent would have to regroup his or her thinking to an entirely new

question area. This increases the respondent burden and produces an inclination to terminate or to inflate the proportion of
nonsubstantive or nondiscriminating responses. Thus, the grouping of questions around a specific variable may make sense to
the researcher, but it is often illogical to the respondent. A
better approach is to group questions according to topic area
for the purposes of the interview and then to rearrange the
items for data analysis.

The second major consideration when contemplating the best
arrangement of question groups is that of implementing transition statements. Transition statements are phrases, words, or
entire sentences that convey a message to the respondent that a
topic change is taking place and that, as a result, the respondent
must shift his or her attention to a new topic. Transitions can
also reduce the problem of response error due to the recall of
answers to previous items by clearly demarcating question con-
texts and suggesting that no relations exist between groups. If it
is necessary to remind a respondent of a certain response, then a
device (for example, a supplemental question form) must be
developed for the interviewer's use. It should be a rare case that
such recall beyond the current question group would be required. Transition statements can also inform a respondent that
the next question will be more complex or that it will require a
little more information to complete. They may contain special
instructions on how the question is to be answered. In addition,
these statements can tell a respondent that a topic is being
considered on another conceptual level, such as moving from
local to national political races. Transitions can take the form of
statements completely separate from questions, initial phrases
of a few words, or complete sentences within the question
wording. Figure 4.6 contains some typical transition statements.
Transitions serve many purposes and should be used liberally
within a questionnaire. They also provide a "sense of movement" through the questionnaire that can be translated as
getting the task completed without causing unnecessary delay
or confusion. The respondent may be less likely to worry about
time if he or she has a feeling that the interview is moving "on

schedule." Finally, transition statements contribute greatly to the ease of administration and response by making a very important contribution to the flow (that is, the relationship) of item groups. This matter is discussed in the next section on question sequence.

QUESTION SEQUENCE

As indicated above, the arrangement of questions should be such that the sequence makes sense to the respondent, maintains respondent interest, is easy to administer, and contributes a sense of organization and legitimacy regarding the research project. In addition to organizational considerations, the problem of question order must be addressed in terms of its potential impact on answer patterns; that is, its role as a source of measurement error or response error.

Transition to New Topic

"Now I would like to ask you some questions about yourself for statistical purposes."

"The next few questions pertain to the state legislature and issues it is currently discussing."

Transition to New Topic and Answer Pattern

"Now I am going to read some statements about political and social issues. I would like you to tell me the extent to which you agree or disagree with these statements. Do you strongly agree . . ."

Transition to New Conceptual Level, Same Topic

"On the national level . . ."

Transition Giving More Information and Facilitating Recall

"As you know, the federal government and the Department of Defense are contemplating locating the MX missile in Nevada. I am going to read you the same list of problems and I would like you to indicate what impact, if any, you feel basing the MX in or near your community will have on each problem."

FIGURE 4.6   Transition Statements

Transition to More Complexity

Question 1 (simple):

"In general, do you feel that those who break the law are being given too light, about right, or too harsh sentences?"

(1) Too light
(2) About right
(3) Too harsh

Question 2 (complex):

"Opinions as to the sentence a convicted offender ought to receive might often vary under certain circumstances. I am going to read a list of some circumstances that might influence the treatment an offender is given, all other things being equal. Please indicate whether you feel that the offender usually should be given a *HARSHER* sentence of a *LIGHTER* sentence in view of each situation described, or whether it should *MAKE NO DIFFERENCE* in your opinion."

	Usually a HARSHER Sentence	Usually a LIGHTER Sentence	Makes No Difference
The offender has a prior record for crime against property.	1	2	3
The offender has a prior record for crime against persons.	1	2	3
The offender is under 21 years of age.	1	2	3
The offender is over 60 years of age	1	2	3
The offender is female.	1	2	3

FIGURE 4.6   Continued

"Question order effect," or "the relative position of an item in an inventory of questions which uniquely influence the manner in which the respondent reacts or answers that question" (Perreault, 1975), has drawn the attention of considerable recent research (Bradburn and Sudman, 1979; Schuman and Presser, 1981; Sigelman, 1981). The focus of this research is the variation in responses that can be attributed to question placement in a survey instrument. Question-order research has begun to look at situations where responses to one item in a survey are consciously or unconsciously influenced by responses to previous items. It is possible that if the original order is reversed or one of the questions not asked, the response pattern may differ. This is called the "consistency effect," which refers to the situation where responses to one item are brought into consistency with responses to earlier items (Bradburn and Mason, 1964). Thus, previous questions can "stack the deck" for later questions.

Schuman and Presser (1981) demonstrated that responses to questions on presidential preference in several Gallup Polls varied by the placement of the question. The same was true for a 1968 poll on Vietnam. Early questions on the United States' justification of its military position contributed to a longer negative evaluation of Johnson as president than what he might have received had the question about his performance as president been asked prior to the Vietnam items. In some cases, early items act as an "anchor" for subsequent responses, creating somewhat of a response set to later items. Unfortunately, a respondent may not answer in terms of a true feeling in his or her attempt to be consistent with earlier judgments (Perreault, 1975). Sigelman (1981) tested for the consistency effect and, though he could not substantiate that it had an effect on response patterns, he was not ready to discount its potential impact.

In addition to the consistency effect, three additional factors of question order can produce response variation. First, after a period of time a respondent begins to wear down, particularly after having answered a series of difficult and/or demanding questions. Respondent fatigue can result in higher item non-response or cryptic, incomplete responses. That is, there is a decline in data quality. The "fatigue effect" can be overcome to some extent by placing easy-to-answer, structured questions near the end of the questionnaire, primarily because respondents are losing their willingness to respond satisfactorily or in necessary detail to questions requiring lengthy responses. At this point, respondents are wearing down and looking forward to the completion of the interview. Hence, items asking for the demographic characteristics of the respondent are better placed near the end of the instrument, since these items usually require familiar, albeit personal, information and are relatively easy to answer. It has been suggested that after six questions of related interest or of similar form, fatigue and subsequent response set begin to take effect (Schuman and Presser, 1981). These can be avoided somewhat by the careful placement of transitions and by variations in question form. These techniques prevent the respondent from becoming too "settled" or bored with the interview.

Responses can also vary if a person feels that questions are repetitive or duplicate previous items. This "redundancy effect" may produce shorter, less detailed responses if the respondent feels that he or she has already responded to an item earlier in the interview. Assuming that there is some potential for confusion, the researcher will have to make clear, either through the use of informational statements or interviewer instructions, that one question is distinct from others previously asked.

The fourth factor that relates to the question order effect is that of *saliency,* which refers to the preparation of the respondent to answer questions of greater complexity or to provide more detailed answers after asking more specific questions earlier on (Bradburn and Mason, 1964; Schuman and Presser, 1981). In this case, the questionnaire is a means of educating the respondent; subsequent answers could be more informed or more biased, depending on the interpretation given the sequence of questions. This has been called the "funnel" or "quintessimal" question sequence (Gallup, 1947) and raises the issue of whether general or specific questions should come first in a particular sequence designed to produce adequate responses to questions of complexity and sensitivity.

There is some debate about the proper sequence for general and specific questions on the same topic. For example, Kalton et al. (1978) asked respondents whether driving standards were getting lower for (a) people in general, and (b) young drivers specifically. When the general question came second, respondents were significantly less apt to say that standards had gone down than when it came first; there was no effect of order on the question about young drivers. This can also be defined as a "contrast effect": After having been asked about young drivers, respondents' views of drivers in general moved further away (in a positive direction) from their views of young drivers. Furthermore, the Kalton et al. (1978) analysis yields a meaningful three-way interaction, since the order effect occurred only for respondents who were themselves classified as older (45+), and who are probably the people most likely to see young drivers as especially reckless. The authors suggest a *subtraction* explanation for the order effect: After answering about young drivers, respondents redefine the general drivers' item to exlude young drivers and, therefore, give a less negative response. Thus, the specific item produced a more refined response to the general item that followed.

Kahn and Cannell (1957) recommend that general questions precede more specific, detailed questions based on the assumption that general questions such as "How would you describe the current energy situation in your county?" or "What do you feel about the current emphasis on back-to-basics in education?" are less likely to influence responses on specific items, but that specific questions create a saliency that could adversely affect responses to subsequent general questions. The movement from general to specific is called the "funnel" technique and is that used most often. The sequence of specific to general questions, or the "inverted" funnel technique, is used when a respondent is likely to have little or no knowledge of the subject area, when an articulated opinion has not been formed, or when it is anticipated that the respondent has such strong feelings on a general topic that detailed questions on a variety of subtopics would elicit bias or undifferentiated responses that would, in turn, be based on opinions expressed in the initial general question.

The effects of the general-specific question order were tested by McFarland (1981). He found no significant question order effect when the placement of general and specific items was varied. There was some evidence for the general preceding the specific, but it was not strong. There was some question order effect with questions on interest (for example, "What is your involvement in politics?"); however, there was no question order effect for items requiring judgment (for example, "How do you feel about the energy crisis?"). It seems that the latter were treated independently by the respondent, although interest questions were not.

There is also some evidence that broad, summary-type questions are more susceptible to contextual redefinition than specific items. The more specific the content of a question and the more concrete the required response, the less the effect of question order; the more vague the question and the required response, the greater the effect of question order. These context effects are also more likely when the researcher attempts to summarize a complex issue into a single item, as this does not allow for specific qualifications within the mind of the respondent. It is better to utilize two or more questions in sequence. Finally, the general-to-specific funnel sequence may be most appropriate early in a questionnaire to "warm up" a respondent; that is, general questions are used first to stimulate the critical faculties of the respondent, thus preparing him or her to respond to more complex, specific questions later. If not warmed up, the respondent is likely to provide incomplete and often socially desirable responses.

Perhaps the greatest relevance of the question order comes with the placement of sensitive questions—those which could embarrass the respondent or cause him or her to be very uncomfortable in providing a response. Premature sensitive questions can produce a "don't know" or a refusal to answer. Before these questions can be presented, trust and rapport need to be established. Waiting to place these items at the end of the questionnaire is also not advisable because of the fatigue factor mentioned above. At this point in the interview, the respondent may simply glide through or even be evasive in order to get through the final phases of the interview. Sensitive items should best be introduced after warm-up material of a less threatening nature has been used and when the asking of a sensitive question makes sense within the context of the larger instrument or within the context of a group of questions.

Finally, I recommend that demographic items, those questions about a respondent's personal characteristics such as age, race, ethnicity, marital status, organizational memberships, and educational achievement, be placed at the end of the questionnaire. These items can be classified as "sensitive," since they do ask for personal information about the respondent; however, resistance to responding accurately or at all to these items is more likely to be overcome, since by this time sufficient rapport between the interviewer and respondent should have been established. That is, the respondent should trust that the interviewer and the purpose of the research are legitimate and that the information required is necessary to the research. Any remaining fear on the part of the respondent can be overcome by a transitional statement marking the change to personal questions and reminding the respondent of the confidential status of his or her responses. For example:

> That concludes our questions on political issues. Now I would like to ask you a few questions about yourself for statistical purposes. Remember, your responses will be kept confidential.

As noted above, it is a mistake to begin with demographic items, since they are sensitive and it is often difficult for the respondent to associate a question on age or race with the research purpose as expressed in the introductory statement. This discrepancy could produce respondent confusion and/or deliberate error on the part of the respondent.

A final argument for placing demographic items in the last phase of the interview is that they are less likely to be affected by respondent fatigue, as these items are relatively easy to answer and do not require arduous recall or answer formulation on the part of the respondent.

Finally, question order provides a context for the interview. This context is altered where questions are rearranged or rotated in and out. One way in which question order effects can be neutralized is, in fact, to use multiple forms of the same questionnaire, each with a different question order. Besides increasing the problems of administration, however, each questionnaire will present a different context; this means that the interviews will not be standardized among respondents. Thus we may create an even greater potential for measurement error by utilizing different question orders. Good interviewing and question writing can overcome some of the difficulties of question order, as can attention to this problem in the pretesting phase. The following list includes some important guidelines for questionnaire design and, more specifically, question-order arrangement.

(1) Treat all questions as part of a whole, not isolated or separate from other items.
(2) The needs of the interviewer, respondent, and coder should all be considered in arranging the questions.
(3) Interviewer error and respondent burden is reduced if the questions "flow" easily one to another.
(4) The question order should permit the interviewer to keep the interview moving at a conversational, yet purposeful pace.
(5) Each question is perceived by the respondent to be in a context of questions. Thus, answers to one question can be affected by responses to others in the same group.
(6) Avoid including items that do not fit into a question context.
(7) The substance of the first question should be consistent with the topic or purpose of research as expressed in the introduction to the interview.
(8) Questions should be grouped according to topic.
(9) Use transitional statements freely.
(10) Be conscious of specific question-order efforts, particularly in arranging general and specific items on the same topic.
(11) Place easy-to-answer items, such as demographic items, at the end of the interview to avoid inadequate responses due to respondent fatigue.
(12) Response set and fatigue can begin to affect responses after six or more items of similar interest or form. Thus, it is a good idea to vary response patterns and group topics as often as is practical.

(13) Avoid questions that duplicate earlier items or appear to the respondent to be redundant.
(14) Place sensitive questions at some point in the middle phase of the interview, after rapport has been established and before fatigue begins to take effect.
(15) Order questions using a logic that will make sense to the respondent.
(16) Precode questions where possible.
(17) Avoid breaking a question between pages of the questionnaire.
(18) Review the questionnaire format with a coder or data processing person.
(19) Clearly distinguish questions from response categories and from instructions to the interviewer.
(20) Pretest the questionnaire on a relevant population using regular interview staff.

Writing Questions

When writing questions, there are innumerable factors to consider. In his classic, *The Art of Asking Questions,* Payne (1951) listed at least 100 items on which to evaluate each question being asked. To apply all of these restrictions to each question would be a formidable task and certainly would present many dilemmas where one factor would be at odds with another. Still, one cannot be casual about question writing, since the question is the vehicle by which researchers obtain desired information and should therefore be as accurate or unbiased as possible. I will discuss several question-writing issues as they relate to telephone survey work, but by no means should this be viewed as an exhaustive treatise. Since many of the considerations of question writing for face-to-face surveys are similar to those for telephone interviews, I suggest that the reader seek additional guidelines on this issue from works such as Payne, 1951; Dillman, 1978; Babbie, 1979; and Schuman and Presser, 1981.

While there are a number of technical considerations in writing questions, this aspect of the research represents a combination of art and science that molds the purpose(s) of the study, the characteristics of the population, and the subtleties of communication with an understanding of the subject matter. Each question has its own logic and must be justifiable in terms of the theoretical or practical problem that stimulated the research. Thus, each question must be "operationalized" into words that mean something to the respondent and that meet research goals. Each questions must also be readable by the interviewer, comprehensible by the respondent, sufficiently structured for the coder, and justifiable in terms of its relation to previous and subsequent questions. More significantly, in telephone research all questions must have the capability of communicating the same meaning (of both words and phrases) to all respondents but with a singular dependence on oral exchanges. This fact complicates question writing for telephone surveys.

Words and phrases are selected to communicate an intent or purpose that has meaning for the respondent. A respondent will be more likely to provide accurate information if the readability of the question is high and if it is comprehensible at his or her level. This means that questions should be written at approximately an eighth-grade level for the general public. At times it is helpful to have a local reading expert apply one of many readability or comprehension scales to your questionnaire. Each item could then be evaluated in a context of this characteristic as it is estimated for the population being studied.

Acknowledging the characteristics of the population, especially expected education level, reduces the potential for writing questions that are vague and that include words that are ambiguous or easily misunderstood. It also reduces the chance of writing questions that assume certain behavior(s) or knowledge on the part of the respondent.

Assessing research goals and determining the nature of the population to be studied in relation to questionnaire design and question writing are especially important when dealing with private, nonacademic clients. Very often, these persons have only a vague or inarticulate idea of their chosen research interest ("We want to know something about child-rearing patterns"), nor do they always have a good grasp of the population that would be most relevant to the study. Very often their original conceptualizations are changed after considerable discussion with the research team. It is therefore a good idea to allow the client to review the proposed questionnaire before it goes into the field. This is for the purpose of classifying any remaining misconceptions of the research goal, not of reviewing the technical organization of the instrument or the writing of questions. In these areas, the researcher refers to his or her expertise and pretests results. It is only on rare occasions that one changes a questionnaire, such as adding a question, at the request of a client once the pretest adjustments have been made and all is ready to begin the calls. Unanticipated changes at the last minute, if serious, can disrupt the continuity or flow of the questionnaire and change the context in which many questions are written. If a client does demand changes, it is better to delay the field phase rather than try to make the adjustment after the training of interviewers and the printing of questionnaires have been completed. If the client persists and the team is about to go into the field, it may be better to determine if the client will fund a second project that will include the items discussed. The following list specifies the criteria that should influence decisions on question selection:

(1) The topic of the question is relevant to the research goal.
(2) The comprehensibility of the question has been established according to characteristics of the relevant population.
(3) The question "fits" in relation to previous or subsequent questions.
(4) The answers obtained in pretests suggest variability in response, not an "all or none" response pattern.
(5) Nonsubstantive responses (for example, "I don't know," or refusals) are at a minimum.
(6) The respondent does not ask the interviewer to explain or rephrase the question.
(7) There are no wording difficulties (for example, bad grammar, incomprehensible slang).

(8) On the face of it at least, the question is a valid measure of a variable or a concept of interest.

(9) The interviewers express no or minimal difficulty in administering the question.

(10) The coders perceive no difficulty recording responses.

(11) The response categories to a closed-ended item are sufficiently exhaustive and mutually exclusive.

(12) The response categories to closed-ended items reflect accurately the classification scheme respondents would utilize in structuring this item or classifying themselves.

(13) The question wording and phrasing are neutral and clearly communicate the intent of question.

(14) The question pertains to only one concept or issue.

(15) The question has the same meaning for researcher, interviewer, coder, and respondent.

(16) The question has survived all pretesting.

QUESTION FORMAT AND RESPONDENT BURDEN: DEALING WITH COMPLEX ITEMS

Telephone interviews, being limited to oral communication between strangers, put severe limits on the nature and substance of the questions that can be asked. It is not possible to use visual aids such as maps, pictures, or cards printed with the appropriate response categories to assist the interviewer, and one cannot be certain that the speed at which the questionnaire is administered matches the respondent's ability to "keep up" and comprehend the questions asked. The basic problem, then, is how to reduce the complexity of telephone questions while at the same time obtaining data of sufficient depth and detail to be meaningful.

Ordinarily, the maxim to "keep it short and simple" is appropriate, but there are times when it is not a desirable guideline (Dillman, 1978). This may be true when the issue being studied is complicated, offering many facets. Very often, respondents need to be informed in some detail of alternative responses to a question before an answer is called for. The result is a lengthy question that has the basic problem of the respondent potentially forgetting the first alternative by the time the third or fourth is read. Dillman (1978) suggests a "Key Word Summary" to assist the respondent. This technique works well as long as that summary is inclusive of all alternatives and does not contain any potentially biasing words or phrases. Figure 4.7 illustrates a key word summary with one of Dillman's (1978) survey items.

A slight change of wording in the summary statement could produce a biased response. If, for example, the summary had read: "Replace them with a burdensome income tax," the proposal would likely to have been opposed by most respondents.

Recently, a proposal to change the kinds of taxes we pay was made in our state legislature. I would like to tell you about this proposal and find out how you feel about it. Here is what it would do.

First, two taxes would be eliminated; these include all special property tax levies for the operation of schools and all sales tax on groceries and prescription drugs.

The money lost would be replaced by a new state graduated income tax that would leave the total amount of taxes collected the same.

Finally, the maximum rate for both the new income tax and the sales tax would be fixed in the state consitution so that neither could be increased except by voter approval.

Key Word
Summary

So, what has been proposed is to eliminate all special property tax levies for schools, and the sales tax on groceries and prescription drugs, and replace them with a state income tax and a sales tax rate fixed in the state constitution.

How do you feel about the proposal? Are you strongly opposed, somewhat opposed, somewhat favorable, or strongly favorable?

(1) Strongly opposed
(2) Somewhat opposed
(3) Somewhat favorable
(4) Strongly favorable

(9) Don't know

Source: Dillman (1978)

FIGURE 4.7   Use of Key Word Summary

The key word summary is an excellent device to assist respondents in remembering the content of the question, but further problems of recall arise with respect to response categories as they are presented in closed-type questions. With too many response categories, the respondent is less likely to remember the proper distinctions and may select a response that does not truly reflect his or her view. This results in what are called response order effects.

Ordinarily, response categories are presented in the same order for each respondent, and the researcher may be unaware that a response order effect is occurring. Schuman and Presser (1981: 77) have identified the "primary" or "recency effect" as the most prominent response order effect. This refers to the tendency for respondents to choose the last or the first alternative, regardless of content. This effect occurs when long lists are used, when rating scales[5] (for example, Agree-Disagree) are implemented, or when any standard closed survey question is utilized. As with question order effects, the research on response order is skimpy, but what is available suggests that response order effects, though important, are not as significant as we might think. On the other hand, too few response categories may mean the lack of a sufficient basis of discrimination among respondents. However, for the sake of respondent burden and reliability, it is better to go with fewer categories, say four or five. These should be transmitted to the respondent as part of the question in order to maintain the continuity and the conversational tone of the interview, as well as to be able to reduce the potential for the respondent being confused on how to answer. Figure 4.8 illustrates this procedure for a single question and for an item that includes a series of responses.

Other adaptations to the requirement of rather detailed distinction on intensity or priority of feelings and attitudes include splitting questions (see Figure 4.9) and using some sort of "unfolding" technique. In the case of splitting a question, the first item is usually of a general nature, where the respondent is asked to state his or her position on an issue—satisfied/dissatisfied, important/not important. Then, depending on the

Single Question

1. Next, I would like to ask you about the desirability of Nevada as a place to live. Do you consider it very desirable, desirable, undesirable, or very undesirable?

   (1) Very desirable
   (2) Desirable
   (3) Undesirable
   (4) Very undesirable
   (9) Don't know/no answer–(DO NOT READ)

Series

1. The federal government is planning to place the MX missile in Nevada. There are several elements that could be affected by the MX should it come to our state. I am going to read a list of several areas of life to you, and I would like you to tell me the extent to which you think the MX will have an effect on each. Do you feel the MX will have a positive, negative, or no impact at all on _____?

                                                              (READ ITEM)

                                                              DO NOT READ

	POSITIVE	NEGATIVE	NO IMPACT	DK	NO ANSWER
(1) Employment	1	2	3	8	9
(2) Education	1	2	3	8	9
(3) Hospital service	1	2	3	8	9
(4) Recreation	1	2	3	8	9
.					
.					
.					
(10) Property values	1	2	3	8	9

(INTERVIEWER: READ RESPONSE CATEGORIES ONLY IF NECESSARY)

   I-A   Of the items mentioned above, which one will be most affected in a negative way? Next most affected negatively?

          Most _____

          Next _____
          (READ LIST OF ITEMS IF NECESSARY)

FIGURE 4.8   Response Categories Within Questions

1. Recently, there has been some discussion of the growth of the population of the city of Las Vegas. Would you like Nevada's population to increase in size, stay about the same, or decrease in size?

>   1—DECREASE
>   2—STAY THE SAME
>   3—INCREASE
>   8—DON'T KNOW   —— (DO NOT READ)
>   9—NO ANSWER

>   (IF INCREASE) Would you like the population to increase at a rate even faster than its current rate, increase at a slower rate, or continue to increase at its current rate?

>   1—FASTER RATE
>   2—SLOWER RATE
>   3—SAME RATE
>   8—DON'T KNOW
>   9—NO ANSWER

FIGURE 4.9   Split Question

answer, a more specific type of question is asked. The split question reduces the potential for confusion and memory failure (Dillman, 1978). It is more desirable to go to some type of split question rather than reduce the number of categories for response, because the former will not result in a loss of information. Indeed, this type of split question technique may be the telephone survey's answer to the inability to use visual aids.

The split question technique is similar to what has been called the "unfolding" tactic (Groves, 1979). In both cases, the major categories of a scale are presented verbally to the respondent, who chooses one alternative. On the basis of this choice, a set of more specific choices are presented for selection. Both techniques were developed to avoid using questions on issues requiring a large number of response categories and to avoid using the hypothetical scale ("on a scale of 0-10, where would you place yourself?"). Sometimes the response pattern is made analogous to a thermometer ("from 0-11 degrees, which would be your feeling?"). Unfortunately, the results have not provided an answer to the problem of being faced with too many response categories. Respondents tend to place themselves on values such as 10°, 50°, or 60° rather than discriminating a position for themselves in between. The result is a variation not unlike what may have been found with the use of four or five response categories.

I favor the split question technique for another reason—it works against "anchoring," or position bias. It has been suggested that when read a large array of response categories, the respondent, particularly when he or she is not sure, will tend to select a consistent category (for example, "When in doubt, take #3"). By being led through an answer sequence, the respondent is not only "informed" on the subject by virtue of an earlier response, but is also given fewer alternatives each time, which makes it easier to respond accurately. Finally, this technique reduces the respondent burden of answering because of the assistance provided and the reduced dependence on memory.

Very often, a researcher may want to obtain a priority ranking of items. This is very easy to accomplish in a face-to-face situation when a respondent can be handed a card with the list of items, or a number of cards with one item listed on each, as in a Q-sort technique. The administration of a question requiring the ranking of items is complicated in a telephone interview by virtue of the fact that the respondent not only must remember the items but mentally keep track of their order or ranking. It is possible for the respondent to do this with three to five items, but it is questionable whether it can be done with more than five; the potential for error due to the inability to remember beyond four or five items is too great.

This problem can be overcome with another version of the split question technique seen in Figure 4.8. In this case, we read the respondent each item and ask for a rating on priority or importance. Then a follow-up question asks the respondent to name the most important, second, and third items from the list. The entire list is read to the respondent if necessary. As Dillman (1978) indicates, this technique does take some additional time to administer, but the loss in time is made up by the gain in information. This type of question has additional possibilities, as an interviewer may ask for elaboration on the highest priority or the lowest, thereby obtaining even more information on an important topic area.

SPECIFIC WORDING PROBLEMS

The complexity of a question can be reduced by the proper choice of words and phrases. Here again, the characteristics of the population are critical. But even with a highly educated population, one related to a specific technical or occupational group, the simpler the language, the smaller the likelihood of misinterpretation. This also means avoiding the use of jargon, slang, technical terms (unless previously explained or of general awareness to the population), abbreviations, and those "ten-dollar" words. Use of more general or simple terms reduces problems of ambiguity and vagueness. Language should not, however, be so simple that it is condescending, but simple enough so that the "typical" respondent can interpret the meaning of the question correctly. Vague words such as "occasionally" or "regularly" should be avoided, as well as other rather imprecise phrases such as "kind of," "sort of," "generally," "in all," or "on the face of it." In addition, one has to be careful that the phrasing of the question does not "lead" a respondent by suggesting that one answer is preferable to another. A question like: "Whom do you favor in the upcoming mayor's election—Mr. Jones, our current mayor who has lowered taxes, or Mr. Smith, the challenger, who would raise taxes?" is clearly suggestive. The use of certain terms like "incumbent" or "liberal" can also predispose a respondent to select a certain answer. These terms are very conversational but subject to multiple interpretations because of their imprecision. More specific guidelines on these problems can be found in many texts on questionnaire design (Payne, 1951; Babbie, 1979; Schuman and Presser, 1981) and do not bear elaboration here. The following list suggests some writing guidelines to follow when drafting questions:

(1) Avoid "loaded" questions that suggest to respondents that one answer is preferable to another.

(2) Avoid the use of inflammatory words such as "Communist," "racist," or "exploitation."

(3) Be natural in wording, but not folksy. Questions should have a conversational tone, written as closely as possible to the manner in which people would talk to each other.

(4) Avoid slang and colloquialisms.

(5) Avoid the use of technical terms and abbreviations that can be misconstrued.

(6) Be precise and specific in the use of concepts (for example, government—is it city, county, or federal?).

(7) Be precise and specific regarding time, either as a period of recall or as a time limit to a certain behavior.

(8) If a question contains facts, make sure they are accurate.

(9) Be careful not to assume behavior or knowledge on the part of any respondent.

(10) Use correct grammar and sentence structure.

(11) Avoid double questions where two (or more) issues are mentioned; split into two questions if necessary.

(12) Response categories must match the dimensions (for example, feeling, or priority) mentioned in question.

(13) Special instructions to the interviewer and respondent should be clear, easily distinguishable, and located on the questionnaire. Instructions to the interviewer are always in "caps."

(14) Wording should be as simple as possible without being condescending to respondent.

(15) Avoid all-inclusive terms such as "never" or "always."

(16) Questions should contain a response category of "don't know" or "no answer/refusal."

(17) Use a technique of splitting a complex question into two or more simpler parts in order to eliminate respondent confusion and error.

(18) Instructions on how to answer should be clearly communicated as part of the question.

Many of the problems with questionnaire design and question

writing can be detected and overcome with the use of a pretest over the phone on respondents similar in characteristics to those who will be part of the final survey. These interviews should be conducted by members of the regular interview staff. The feedback will obviously be helpful in evaluating the questionnaire. Before the final questionnaire is written, however, the pretest results should also be compared to final evaluations by the coder and other members of the field work staff. Even this will not provide the perfect testing instrument, but there should be considerably less difficulty in its administration.

It is true that questionnaire design and question writing, whether for face-to-face, mail, or telephone surveys, represent a combination of art and science. In the case of the telephone survey, the last five years have seen a move by telephone questionnaire design from a larger representation in the "art" category to a more substantial position with "science." That is, the techniques of writing questions and designing questionnaires are based more today on proven, demonstrable techniques than on survey folklore. The same contention can be made about the administration of telephone surveys, the subject of the next chapter.

Notes

1. Response effects refer to error (i.e., deviation from the true answer) produced by factors that intervene between the asking of the question and the giving of an answer (Sudman and Bradburn, 1974). Thorough discussions of response effects are available, but again, these treatments reflect nontelephone experiences. Face-to-face surveys (Deming, 1944; Phillips, 1971; Sudman and Bradburn, 1974) and research experiments (Rosenthal, 1966) provide the background for most analyses of response effects. Schuman and Presser (1981) have recently published a comprehensive monograph on the effects of question form, wording, and context on responses. This text provides an analysis of question-related sources of response effects based on several experiments in question design.

2. Obviously, this is not always true, as telephone calls can be placed to respondents to inform them that a questionnaire is coming in the mail, or letters can be sent to a telephone sample to apprise them of an upcoming call. The latter will work only where lists are available, and it cannot be used with surveys utilizing random digit dialing.

3. The "foot-in-the-door" technique involves a two-step procedure whereby a respondent is initially asked to complete a small task; later, the same subject is asked to perform a larger, more time-consuming task. Most data on the effectiveness of this technique are developed from the experimental studies, and not studies based on probability samples. A summary of this research can be found in DeJong (1979).

4. Question order should be distinguished from response order, which refers to the sequencing or arranging of response categories to closed-type questions.

5. Schuman and Presser (1981) suggest that a portion of the acquiescence response tendency can be explained not by the bias toward "agreeing," but by the primary effect, since the "agree" alternative is usually placed first, even when question intent is reversed. Their one experiment on this phenomenon did not support this notion, however.

CHAPTER 5

ADMINISTRATION

Some of the major advantages of telephone surveys can be found in their administration or implementation. This is particularly true with respect to quality control, or the ability to manage the field work factors associated with asking questions and recording answers. These factors have the potential to produce error or imperfections in the finished product (that is, the interview data).

In the case of surveys, the major sources of bias involve questionnaire construction, sample selection, and questionnaire implementation. The design of the questionnaire is no better than the experience and ability of the project director or team constructing the instrument and, except for some technical adaptations to survey mode, there are no inherent characteristics in any particular type of survey that can improve upon deficiencies in design capabilities. However, the sample selection and questionnaire implementation phases can be monitored more closely for telephone surveys. The advent of such technical innovations as random digit dialing (RDD) number selection, Computer-Assisted Telephone Interviewing (CATI), and phone-monitoring systems makes it possible to exercise greater control over the selection of numbers, the timing of callbacks, and the art of interviewing than is possible in other types of surveys. Even if one does not have the assistance of a computer, locating the interviewing in a centralized facility improves quality control by providing controlled sample selection through systematic number assignment to interviewers, as well as continuous supervision, either through the presence of a supervisor or by technical monitoring of the administration of virtually every interview.

Thus, not only does the telephone survey offer the administrative advantage of low cost because of reduced travel time for the initial contact and call-backs, it also provides control over the two most significant sources of survey error—respondent selection and interviewer mistakes. The sampling techniques associated with telephone interviewing have already been discussed in considerable detail (see Chapter 3). This chapter will review the administrative tasks necessary for the administration of a telephone survey, with particular reference to controlling the implementation of the questionnaire. Certainly there is more to administration than supervising the field work. However, I do not feel it necessary to discuss in any detail matters such as negotiating contracts, writing grants, implementing sample design, supervising design phases and pretests, and organizing statistical analyses. In some cases, these are discussed in previous chapters (for example, sampling and questionnaire design). Other tasks, such as grant writing or statistical analysis, while the responsibility of the administrator or project director, have well-known guidelines available from other sources. I intend to concentrate on the field implementation of the telephone questionnaire, an area in need of standardization and additional direction.

The Administrative Plan

Once the research problem has been defined and the decision to pursue a telephone survey has been made, it is necessary to develop an administrative plan or procedure outlining the sequence of tasks, including their timing and the personnel required, that must be followed in order for the survey to be completed. Figure 5.1 shows a typical sequential plan for telephone survey administration.[1] Variations in this plan are determined by the monies available for the project, and/or by the nature of the sampling (RDD or directory listing). However, I would assert that regardless of the research timetable, all of the tasks included here must be completed in any properly run survey. It is probably not necessary for a survey director to map out a flow chart similar to the one presented here for each survey he or she administers, since many of the tasks and their timing sequence are well known.

ACTIVITY CHECKLIST

Every survey project is sufficiently different in detail and personnel that it is necessary to prepare some kind of activity checklist for each one. This is the case regardless of the experience of the research team or the sophistication of the technology available for the project. The activity checklist contains a detailed listing of various tasks and activities, along with a way to designate who is responsible and when each activity is to take place. Figure 5.2 provides a sample checklist of activities like those used at the Las Vegas Telephone Survey Center of the University of Nevada. When a contract is signed for a telephone survey project, this list is utilized to specify responsibility and timing. It is reviewed daily by the project director and/or the research team to determine progress on each major task and minor activity. Of course, the fact that work will be occurring on many activities simultaneously is even a better reason for having some device available to monitor the administrative process. Pertinent information, such as who is responsible or any anticipated complications, is included in the "Comments" column, and the "Ready" column contains indications of the completion status of each activity.

BUDGET

In addition to the survey checklist, the budget represents another significant source of project control. The contract amount is usually based on an agreement reached with the client or sponsor. This figure is largely determined by two factors—sample characteristics and interview length. It is rela-

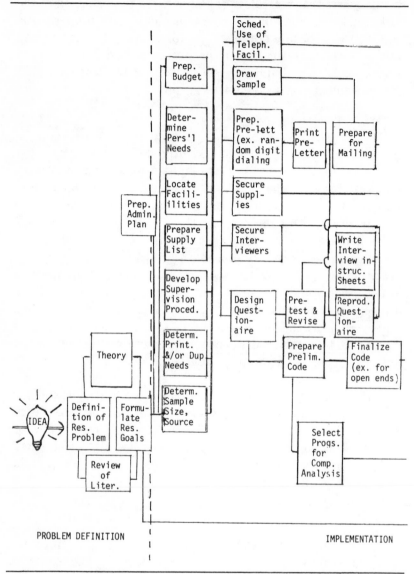

FIGURE 5.1   Telephone Survey Tasks

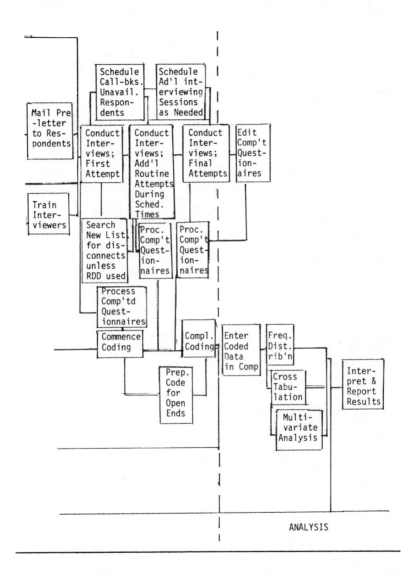

ANALYSIS

Project: _____   Begin date: _____

Sponsor: _____

Project Amt. $ _____   Completion date: _____

Project Director(s) _____

ITEM	COMMENTS	READY

A. Project timetable established
   (1) Interviewer training
   (2) Sample selection
   (3) Interviewing begins
   (4) Report due
   (5) Other key times

B. Survey center facility
   (1) Reserved for calling
   (2) Equipment working

C. Personnel requirements
   (1) Operations supervisor(s)
   (2) Interveiwers
   (3) Coder(s)
   (4) Programmer
   (5) Keypunch operator
   (6) Other

D. Budget preparation
   (1) Contract amount verified
   (2) Accounts and budget control
        procedure established
   (3) Itemized budget prepared
   (4) Other

E. Interviewers
   (1) Recruiting commenced
   (2) Training materials ready
   (3) Training scheduled
   (4) Employment contracts
      −Employment referral form
      −Employee time cards
      −W-4 forms
      −Time sheets

FIGURE 5.2

F. Supplies
   (1) Phone books (if necessary)
   (2) Pencils
   (3) Staples
   (4) Pencil sharpeners
   (5) Other

G. Sampling and calling
   (1) Exchange proportions
       determined
   (2) Random numbers selected
   (3) Number assignment forms
   (4) Call tally form
   (5) Interviewer calling summary
   (6) Preletter ready (if necessary)
   (7) Preletter mailed
   (8) Other

H. Questionnaire
   (1) Pretest
   (2) Printed and assembled
   (3) Assignment forms
   (4) Special instructions posted

I. Data Analysis
   (1) Code book
   (2) Item code
   (3) Coding forms
   (4) Computer program written
   (5) Computer access established

J. Other
   (1) Survey info to switchboard
   (2) Survey info to infor office
   (3) Survey info to departments
   (4) Other publicity

FIGURE 5.2   Continued

tively easy to determine sample size, sample accessibility, and
the geographical boundaries of the sample in advance of actual
implementation; this is not the case with interview length. Most
clients are specific about whether a local, regional, or national
sample is desired and whether the sample is to be of the general
public or a specialized group. The researcher can then provide

some estimate of sampling precision, which will then convert to an agreeable sample size given the scope and nature of the sample population.

Determining the interview length is another matter. The number of questions has a significant impact on interviewer and supervisory wages, two very significant costs in a survey budget. Any project director can usually give a cost-per-interview estimate based on a certain sample size and scope, and on his or her experiences with various interview lengths. For example, we have found that a 10-minute questionnaire for a local survey of 350 residents costs approximately $7.50 per completed interview. A statewide survey of approximately 600 residents will cost approximately $15-$18 per completed interview, and a national survey of approximately 2000 members of the general public around $25-$30 per completed interview.[2] Estimates can be based on the anticipated length, but until one actually constructs a pretest questionnaire and administers it for time and construction factors, it is difficult to anticipate interviewing costs accurately. Since one does not usually have the luxury of a pretest before offering a projected contract amount, it is important to know how much a client has available for the project, and his or her research needs. At least this provides an upper budgetary limit and an idea of how many questions will be necessary to fulfill the client's information needs before cost projections are formulated.

A frequent problem in contract negotiations arises when a client wants to expand question areas after the contract amount has been determined. I remember negotiating a survey with a political group (possibly the worst offenders in this regard) to conduct a statewide survey with an instrument that would require approximately 5-7 minutes to administer. Just before the interviewing phase was to begin, however, they expressed a desire to obtain additional information which would have meant doubling the administration time of the questionnaire. Naturally, they were not prepared to increase the contract amount, nor were they willing to compromise on the sample size. The final result, after considerable argumentation, was the addition of only two items.

Figure 5.3 depicts a form used in project budget preparations at the Survey Center of the University of Nevada, Las Vegas. This device is used for budget projections and/or financial guidelines for each project. It is necessary to maintain standard accounting practices for each item (interviewer wages, fringes, overhead, and the like) of the budget. In addition, most commercial firms and academic institutions will be able to provide the services of an accountant and/or computerized budget control supervision. Continuous monitoring of the budget is necessary, since research decisions such as sample size adjustments, call-back scheduling, interviewer utilization, and facility scheduling are often contingent on budgetary considerations.

Specific costs of facility utilization, interviewer wages, supervisory expenses, and overhead are determined by local markets. We will pay interviewers from $4.50 to $7.50 per hour using a sliding scale based on experience and budget limitations. There is no evidence that productivity is enhanced by paying on a piece-rate or per-completion basis. I do not recommend this approach, since it often produces hurried, sloppy work. Supervisors receive between $7.00 and $8.50 per hour. Facility utilization and other overhead costs are determined in consultation with the major budget officials of the institution. In some cases, indirect costs can be as high as 110 percent of wages, salaries, and fringe benefits. Local and long distance phone costs can be calculated with some accuracy once interview length and sample size have been determined. One final caveat: There is often a tendency for project directors, particularly those in academia, to underprice their expertise. They usually think this puts them in a favorable light with clients and that it will mean future business. It is my view that this type of compromise only demeans the survey and the skills of the researcher. Most clients are more than willing to pay established fees at the going market rate. In fact, the more they pay, the better they feel about the expertise they are acquiring. As the director of a

Project: _____

Contracting Party:

    Name or Organization: _____

    Address: _____

    Phone: _____

Dates contract to be effective: _____

Type of survey desired: _____

                      (Mail, telephone, household)

Questionnaire length: _____Pages   _____ Minutes

Type of sample: _____ Sample size _____

Geographical area coverage: _____

Number of interviewing days: _____

ITEM	COST
A. Phone usage ($5.00 per day per line, eight (8) phones available)	$ _____
B. Interviewer wages ($ ____per hr. x ____hrs.)	_____
C. Support staff wages (keypunch, coder, sampling) ($ ____per hr. x ____hrs.)	_____
D. Project coordinator wages ($ ____per hr. x ____hrs.)	_____
E. Clerical ($ ____per hr. x ____hrs.)	_____
F. Fringe benefits (1% of b+c+d)	_____
G. Professional services: UNLV faculty time ($ ____per hr. x ____hrs.)	_____
H. Professional Services: Consultants ($ ____per hr. x ____hrs.)	_____
I. Travel	_____
J. Suppleis (paper, training, materials, etc.)	_____
K. Long distance phone charges	_____
L. Duplicating and mailing costs	_____
M. Data processing-computer time	_____
N. Other _____	_____
TOTAL ESTIMATED COST	$ _____

FIGURE 5.3   Project Cost Estimates

rather small research operation, I budget any project, regardless of scope, for a minimum of two days at $300 per day for professional services, because I know that even the smallest survey will require that much time and attention from myself or consultants. These costs are largely consumed in the initial phases of the project where, along with other staff, the professional consultant works on questionnaire and sampling design. Any projection in wages should include costs associated with pre-field work preparation, as well as with the actual interview phase.

The administrative plan with an activity checklist and a budget provides a significant source of project control. This is not, however, peculiar to telephone surveys. Quality control in telephone research has been enhanced in recent years by three developments: the centralized facility, increased monitoring capabilities, and Computer-Assisted Telephone Interviewing (CATI).

Quality Control

CENTRALIZED LOCATION

Prior to the early 1960s, telephone interviewing used to be a "cottage industry," where calls were made from the homes of the interviewers (Blankenship, 1977). This meant that telephone surveys had some of the same quality control problems found in face-to-face surveys. The lack of close supervision created problems in correcting interviewer error, clarifying respondent inquiries, and verifying interviewer completion. These problems were largely alleviated by the development of the centralized telephone interviewing facility.

The first centralized facility was introduced by Sanford Cooper of Burke, Inc. in the 1950s and has been adopted by most academic and commercial survey organizations. Its utilization was enhanced by the development of the Wide Area Telecommunications Service (WATS), which made it possible to conduct national surveys from a central location. The centralized facility usually contains 8-15 telephone stations. Each station or booth, soundproofed in some fashion, contains only a desk, information for interviewers, writing utensils, and a telephone, preferably with a headset. The telephones should be of the push-button variety rather than rotary dial, since the former work twice as fast and are less fatiguing. While usually a permanent fixture, telephone facilities can be established on a temporary basis, though this is not usually cost effective, since installation is very expensive. The centralized facility may appear to be an old-fashioned "boiler room" where several callers, located in one room, are soliciting fraudulent stock and security sales. However, in contrast to the boiler room operation, which attempted to create the perception in the mind of the respondent that the background "buzz" emanated from a brokerage house rather than a clandestine back room, the centralized telephone facility has no other purpose than to provide a location for survey work. In fact, the background noise of a telephone survey may contribute to the legitimacy of that survey, since the respondent can be comforted by the fact that others are receiving calls and that this particular call is not from some isolated location and is therefore not likely to be a crank call.

There are many additional advantages to utilizing a centralized facility. The following list represents only a partial summary of these:

(1) A central location makes it possible for all interviewers to be represented within all sample segments. Interviewers can be assigned randomly to calling areas, thereby controlling for interviewer variance over different regions (Eastlak and Assael, 1966).

(2) Sample reliability is more easily obtainable, since it is easier to monitor completion among prescribed proportions (such as sex or age) for a stratified random sample; on-the-spot adjustments can be made if necessary.

(3) Quality control, particularly in the form of interviewer supervision, is easier to establish. The physical presence of a supervisor and/or the placement of a monitoring device at each station will permit continuous assessment of interviewing style, the ability to

follow instructions, and probing quality. Thus, the opportunity for "on-the-job training" (OJT) and for continuous interviewer development is facilitated by a centralized setting. It is also possible to distinguish interviewers who have special qualities that may be usable for other phases of the interviewing process (for example, converting refusals), and to identify weak interviewers who may have to be terminated early in the interview phase.

(4) Quality control is also enhanced by the availability of "immediate feedback" in a centralized location. This can take the form of correcting faults and praising accomplishments on the part of interviewers. It is also possible for the supervisor, or even the project director, if available, to respond to questions from both respondents and interviewers. Finally, recording mistakes can be corrected, since editing takes place at the completion of each interview. The latter may also serve as an additional motivation for interviewers, since they know their work is being evaluated immediately.

(5) Should unanticipated problems arise, the project director can immediately institute corrective adjustments to the interview schedule. It is then possible to improve or delete poor questions, revise a difficult question sequence, or solve other problems that did not arise during the pretest.

(6) Areas can be identified where training was inadequate and where more education is needed.

(7) It is easy to monitor sample selection and call-backs. This is particularly valuable where household member selection procedures are being instituted.

(8) Researchers are able to monitor responses and can gain a sense of whether or not the questions being used are obtaining the desired data (Lucas and Adams, 1977).

(9) It is possible to reassign some interviews to more adept interviewers or to those who are excellent at converting refusals or reaching new numbers in an efficient manner (Dillman, 1978).

(10) Interviewers are not exposed to physical risk.

(11) Interviewers can learn from each other.

(12) All interviews can be verified as complete.

(13) It is easier to control the distribution and collection of interviewing materials and interview schedules.

(14) Fewer persons are required for the project, particularly at the supervisory level.

As the list clearly demonstrates, the major advantages of a centralized facility rest with quality control, particularly with the ability to correct for interviewer error, and with cost reduction as expressed in personnel requirements and supervisory travel costs. It is difficult to imagine any telephone survey of quality being conducted from a facility other than one that was centralized.

WATS LINES

The increased use of centralized telephone interview locations was paralleled by the development of the Wide Area Telecommunications Service, or WATS.[3] This system, first made available in the middle 1960s by Illinois Bell, provides the opportunity for a bulk user, such as a survey center, to purchase telephone time covering various areas of the country at discount prices. The phone company does not bill the user for individual calls, but rather establishes a bulk rate based on an agreed-upon number of hours of use. For example, a user may contract for 500 hours per month at a certain rate. The rate structures are available from the local or regional phone company. If the user exceeds the established contract hours, an additional fee is charged, though still at a reduced rate. It is estimated that WATS saves the user approximately one-third the charges that would be incurred with standard direct dialing procedures. It is important to note, however, that the bulk rate is charged regardless of the number of hours used. If the user has contracted for 500 hours per month and only uses 250, the user still pays the 500-hour rate. This is why it is important to schedule interviews so as to make maximum use of the survey facility and the WATS rates. Thus, WATS is most valuable to those users with a large number of survey contracts.

The rates are also prorated by geographical band areas. Area 1 is the state; in this case, Nevada; area 2 comprises the most contiguous states to Nevada, such as California, Arizona, Utah, and Oregon. Areas 3-6 represent states at a greater distance from Nevada. These rates will be subject to considerable change over the next few years since the telecommunications industry has now been deregulated, and appeals for rate changes no longer have to be made to the State Public Service Commissions.

MONITORING OF INTERVIEWS

In the late 1950s, several commercial firms, namely Chilton and Sindlinger, began monitored central location interviewing (Blankenship, 1977). Today, most survey organizations have developed some type of mechanical method to overhear any interview being conducted. A supervisor located within a centralized facility cannot possibly supervise adequately all of the interviews taking place, but by using a listening device, he or she can patch into an interview without a warning signal and listen to its progress. In some cases the supervisor will simultaneously record respondent replies for later comparison with those recorded by the interviewer. Those who have a CATI system can actually plug into the interview schedule as it appears on an interviewer's CRT and duplicate the material on a CRT located at the adjacent supervisory facility.

There is considerable controversy, of course, about the two-way monitoring of phone conversations, even when it is done for survey purposes. It is possible to circumvent these concerns by offering a disclaimer as part of the informed consent procedure, where a segment of the introductory statement declares that the interview may be monitored for the sake of supervision only. Thus, permission to complete the interview is also taken to be permission to listen in on the interview. In any case, quality control in the form of efficient questionnaire administration and reduced interviewer error is improved by monitoring activities that go beyond exclusive dependence on the abilities of an operations supervisor physically located within the centralized interviewing facility.

COMPUTER-ASSISTED TELEPHONE INTERVIEWING (CATI)

Even with the rapid developments that had occurred in telephone survey research, there continued to be some concern with controlling the interview process and interviewer-respondent interactions (Shure and Meeker, 1978). In addition, surveying large populations and screening to specialized subgroups were discouraged because of cost considerations and the burden such tasks placed on all phases of survey operations (Shanks et al., 1981). Finally, even though telephone surveys provide the quickest data retrieval and reporting time, in our fast and furious world a wait as short as a few days can make data irrelevant, particularly to policymakers who need immediate feedback on a potential action. Paper-and-pencil or manual telephone surveys were proving to be inefficient with large surveys; they also experienced an inordinate amount of interviewer error, particularly when a number of screen or filter questions were used, and very often the paper-and-pencil survey was too time consuming. CATI was developed in response to these problems.

The first commercial CATI system was developed by Chilton in 1972; it is called the Survey Processor System (Fink, 1981). The prototype academic system was developed shortly thereafter at the Institute for Social Science Research at the University of California at Los Angeles (UCLA). Most existing CATI systems are modeled after one of these founding systems. At this writing, about a dozen commercial and academic organizations have or are developing a CATI system. These include the commercial firms of Chilton, Audits and Surveys; MARC, Inc.; Amrigon, Inc., as well as the academic institutions of UCLA, the University of California at Berkeley, the University of Michigan, and the University of Wisconsin. In addition, the U.S. Bureau of the Census and the U.S. Department of Agriculture are exploring the possibility of establishing a CATI system for their own use. So great is the interest in CATI that a research and development group in Computer-Assisted Survey Methods (CSM) has been formed under the auspices of the Berkeley Survey Research Center. This group is establishing cooperative agreements with many survey organizations, including those desiring CATI capabilities but unable to afford the costs of installation and maintenance of the equipment necessary to operate a CATI system.

Under a CATI system, all interviewing is done at a CRT terminal where, instead of penciling responses on to pages, the interviewer keys them into a CRT. The interview is actually controlled by preprogrammed machine processes. Thus, in effect, the respondent talks to the computer through the interviewer. CATI directs the flow of each interview and instantaneously provides the interviewer with exactly the right question— one question at a time. Preprogrammed editing instructions work to ensure that the responses are valid and consistent with answers to previous questions. If an interviewer keys in an inappropriate response (for example, not included in response categories), an error message automatically appears on the screen and corrective measures can be implemented immediately. When the correct response is entered, the computer determines which question should be asked next. The next question will not appear until the previous question has been answered with an appropriate response category. At the end of the interview, all respondent replies are automatically and instantaneously entered into the computer memory.

CATI systems are usually installed in centralized locations containing soundproof booths equipped with a CRT, telephone, desk, headset, and chair. The computer is located in an adjoining room, as are the supervisors, who utilize a video monitor for each interviewer. Interviewers activate their stations by logging on with name and identification number, as well as some interviewer classification such as "regular," "bilingual," or "refusal converter" (Fielder, 1979). Interviewers are then presented with a number to dial. This number is computer-generated; it is not assigned by the supervisor as is the case in paper-and-pencil studies. The number is then followed by a series of possible response codes such as "ineligible," "busy," or "no answer." Depending on the outcome of the dialing, the interviewer enters a code for calling back, trying again, designating the number as invalid, or proceeding with the interview. Questions and responses automatically appear on the screen.

Branching is handled by the computer, making it unnecessary for the interviewer to read and follow written instructions. In sum, the interview proceeds with the computer handling question order, question or response category rotation, branching or filtering sequences, within-household respondent selection, initial number or respondent randomization and selection, and response validation or editing.[4] By permitting the computer to control these functions, the two most significant advantages of CATI are illustrated—respondent selection control and reduced interviewer error.

CATI, by controlling the standard interview process through specifying question order, response format and checks, and branching instructions, eliminates most interviewer error associated with skipping or overlooking items and with recording inappropriate responses. This capability also reduces post-interview costs associated with interview validation and call-backs. When the more complex functions of the interview process, such as respondent selection, branching, and question sequence are performed by the computer, the interviewer is left free to concentrate on asking the question on the CRT display and establishing rapport with the respondent (Fielder, 1979). The advantages of CATI are summarized in the following list:

(1) List randomization or question rotation are performed by the computer, thus relieving the interviewer of the task of selecting a random start or dealing with several forms of the same instrument. CATI permits the assessment of order effects.

(2) CATI aids interviewer and respondent recall. Interviewers do not need to remember anything said previously, since the computer provides the necessary screening or sequencing. The computer will also produce an earlier answer or stored information necessary for response to a subsequent item.

(3) Consistency checks over the course of an interview in order to detect response sets or discrepancies in respondent replies are readily applied.

(4) CATI is capable of registering interviewer comments and associating these with certain questions.

(5) CATI assists the recording and coding of responses to open-ended responses by offering standardized probes or the immediate translation of a response to an item code scheme.

(6) Automatic calling list updates for the administration of sampling and respondent selection are possible. Call-backs, retries, and appointment call-backs automatically come up at designated and, if necessary, at randomized times.

(7) CATI enables researchers to undertake complex surveys requiring intricate branching or extremely sophisticated sampling.

(8) Immediate feedback can be obtained on sample status by monitoring completion rates, optimal times for calling, and interviewer completion rates. This information can be used for efficient scheduling.

(9) Keypunching functions can be virtually eliminated, thereby reducing these costs. This is called Direct Data Entry (DDE), and some difficulties remain with its operationalization.[5]

(10) Limits on sample size are not necessary, at least in a practical sense.

(11) CATI provides up-to-the-minute tabulations.

Perhaps the most significant advantage of CATI, beyond those of respondent selection and lowered interviewer error, will be that of increasing the opportunities for research on survey methods (Shanks, 1981). Systematic experimental research on survey practices, including instrument design, interviewer training, and question writing, are more possible with CATI than with paper-and-pencil surveys, which usually do not provide the flexibility to conduct such investigations. At this time, however, developmental or software problems prevent the implementation of such manipulations.

CATI is not without its problems. As you might expect, there can be hardware failures that result in computer down time and effective stoppage of the survey. There is even the potential for core data disc damage and the resultant loss of previously gathered data—a project director's nightmare. Thus, it is a good idea to have the paper-and-pencil alternative available in case a mechanical breakdown results in prolonged down time.

The second greatest disadvantage is that of operator error. Here again, the interviewer is the source of the problem. He or she may make inappropriate entries that are not instantly detectable, but that cause considerable editing and coding problems later. To avoid this, interviewer training on CATI is usually more extensive and more costly than training for manual surveys.

Setting up a CATI system and preparing for a survey on CATI is more time consuming and costly than preparing for a paper-and-pencil survey. UCLA and Berkeley researchers took nearly eight months to get ready for the California Disability Study (Shanks et al., 1981), and even then they were not able to anticipate all of the problems, so that considerable debugging effort was expended. Installing the hardware for a CATI system usually calls for an outlay of approximately $100,000, a sum not available to many survey operations. This factor alone suggests that cooperative agreements among survey firms (such as sharing CATI facilities) merit serious consideration. However, experience with micro systems such as the one at the University of Wisconsin suggests that computerized interviewing is possible for a considerably smaller expenditure on hardware costs.[6]

Originally, there was some concern over "machine fear" on the part of interviewers and of resistance to conversing with a computer on the part of respondents. Both appear not to be a problem. Once the initial insecurity of utilizing the CRT is overcome, interviewers tend to prefer it because of the reduced complexity of their task. Field directors have not noted an unusual refusal rate with CATI surveys, either. Respondents appear to understand that their responses will eventually reach a computer anyway, and that responding to a computer-controlled interview accentuates its confidentiality (Fielder, 1979).

CATI systems are still very much in the developmental phase, particularly with the software component in such areas as appropriate language translations (Klecka, 1981). While such a system has considerable advantages, it is still only available to the larger and more resourceful academic and commercial survey firms, except where corporate agreements can be established. Perhaps until microcomputers are available with appropriate programming input, most survey research operations will continue to use the paper-and-pencil alternative, to which most of the following will apply.

Interviewing

As indicated in the previous selection, interviewer error is of significant concern to telephone survey researchers. Data quality can be severely compromised by inaccurate recording of responses, improper attention to probing and clarification instructions, skipping questions, or posing questions that "lead" or unduly influence a respondent's answer. General discussions of interviewing pitfalls and their avoidance are discussed expertly elsewhere (Babbie, 1979; Gorden, 1980; Backstrom and Hursh-Cesar, 1981). Research reports on sources of interviewer error include those by Bailer et al. (1977) and Blair (1979); however, the results of this research, including that on interviewer background or personality comparisons, have generally been inconclusive. As a result, recruitment, training, and supervision still remain the keys to controlling interviewer error.

RECRUITING

In most cases telephone interviewers are women who have been recruited by referral or advertisement. Some men are successful at interviewing, but their participation is not as great, since their work schedules tend to preclude their availability during daytime calling hours. The fact that most survey directors seem to prefer female interviewers may reflect the feeling that a woman is less likely to obtain a refusal than a male, although the evidence suggests that this is not the case (Dillman et al., 1976). In addition, women are more likely to be available for interviewing, since it is an occupation that often calls for short-term, sporadic employment and that fulfills the preference of many women for part-time work.

It is advisable to build an interviewer pool from which a project director can draw qualified and experienced personnel. When this reserve is exhausted, it is necessary to recruit persons who have not had experience at your (or any other) survey facility. In some areas, such as urban communities or college towns, it is relatively easy to locate enough people to complete an interviewer pool. Even then, however, there is no guarantee that those who might want to be interviewers have the necessary qualifications or are able to conduct acceptable interviews.

The characteristics of a good telephone interviewer have yet to be defined. However, based on their experience with various surveys and many interviewers, project directors can depend on their senses, if nothing else, to select the people who will make good interviewers. In addition to these subjective judgments, others have developed screening procedures as part of the interviewer selection process. This usually means conducting a practice interview, first face-to-face, and then with a phone interchange. The first factor to consider is voice quality. The tone of voice must be such that it can be heard clearly over the telephone, even when there is telephone noise, which is often encountered with long distance calls. It should be free of any heavy accent, harshness, or other irritating qualities that could make it difficult to understand or to listen to comfortably over a long period of time. Finally, the voice should not be irritating to other interviewers, nor so loud that it could override other interviewers. We once had an interviewer with a very good telephone voice but bothersome to fellow interviewers. Since this person was a successful interviewer with very few refusals, we were able to assign her to a calling station separate from the centralized facility. This should only be done, however, when the interviewer is experienced and can be trusted to follow instructions without deviation. A prospective interviewer's voice can and should be tested by actual phone conversations or by having someone who does not know the prospective interviewer listen and judge the voice (Dillman, 1978).

It is also important to have interviewers who can read well and follow a question sequence without unusually long or unnecessary pauses. This characteristic can be tested by having a prospective interviewer administer a relatively uncomplicated set of questions to the person doing the hiring. Some firms will ask prospective interviewers to administer a questionnaire of some length, but I am not sure this is productive or even fair, since in most cases the person has not been trained to do telephone interviewing, nor has he or she had any experience. Thus, administering a 3-4-page questionnaire, even of the simplest form, may not be the best technique for judging interviewer quality.

Not only should interviewers be able to read well, they should also be able to record accurately. This means being able to follow instructions and make appropriate remarks while simultaneously guiding respondents through the interview in a smooth and flowing fashion.

Naturally, interviewers should have good work habits such as dependability, motivation to be productive, ability to follow directions, initiative, and self-confidence. The latter is especially important when interviewers receive unanticipated questions such as: "How did you get my number?" and must then "think on their feet." This trait cannot usually be tested in advance, but it is one that project directors and supervisors should look for in interviewer performance. Often, those who show exceptional capability in this area make good supervisors, provided that they also have some success in interview completion.

Telephone interviewing can be tedious, burdensome work. There are not many people who can initiate and maintain a conversation with a stranger; who can simultaneously read questions, record answers, follow instructions, and concentrate to the point of ruling out distractions from others nearby; and who are task-directed and yet have the ability to respond in a pleasant and consistent fashion to all types of persons and all types of questions. It may not be until an interviewer is actually at work that a project director or supervisor is able to judge his or her true quality. This is one of the benefits of a centralized telephone facility where poor interviewers can be detected almost immediately and some corrective action taken, either more training or termination, before serious damage is done. The best recruiting may be done once a study is underway, when judgments on interviewer quality can be based on direct observation rather than subjective prior assessments.

For any given study, it is a good idea to have a pool of interviewers available that is at least twice the size of the number of phones that will be utilized. For example, the Telephone Survey Center at the University of Nevada, Las Vegas, houses eight phones, while an interview pool of 14-16 interviewers is hired for any study conducted at the center. The excess supply of interviewers is necessary to be able to cover all scheduled calling hours. Many persons who are "moonlighting" will only be available at certain hours. Housewives may only be able to work during the times a babysitter is available. Finally, given the demands of the interviewing task, few are willing or able to work more than a four-hour shift at any one time, nor are they willing to work several nights running. In fact, we will not schedule an interviewer for more than four hours at any one time and insist that the interviewer take at least two 10-minute breaks during that time. For surveys with especially large sample sizes, it is advisable to hire *three* times the number of phones available in order to cover all necessary working shifts.

One final note on recruiting: There are many persons who say they can interview based on some experience as a phone solicitor for magazines, house insulation, or the like. Certainly, having been a phone solicitor makes it easier to call strangers, but it does not necessarily qualify one as an interviewer. We have often found that persons with phone solicitation experience are brash with respondents, more likely to vary from instructions and, in their motivation to be productive (that is, to get the completed interview), prone to rush through an interview at a pace uncomfortable to the respondent and sure to produce response error. Thus, even those with phone solicitation experience need the same training and supervision as any other interviewer—perhaps more so.

TRAINING

There is no predominant pattern to interviewer training. Some firms will spend three days educating interviewers on all phases of the upcoming survey; others will take only a few hours. Generally, CATI system surveys will require additional time compared to the paper-and-pencil variety because of the need to learn operational procedures involving a CRT and preprogrammed question and instruction patterns. Naturally, less time may be taken in training more experienced interviewers.

In general, training occurs in three phases: general, study-specific, and operational. During the first phase, interviewers are instructed on general interviewing techniques such as probing, following question and wording sequences, eliciting compliance, pacing, pronunciation, and question presentation, as well as how to adopt a rapport-establishing conversational tone while at the same time guiding the respondent through the task of completing the questionnaire. This is what we call a "balanced rapport." During this phase, special characteristics of telephone interviewing are discussed, such as the total reliance on oral communication. This is also a time for the use of video tapes and role-playing to assess interviewing style. Figures 5.4 and 5.5 provide some typical guidelines for topics discussed during this phase. Of course, this initial phase may be curtailed, or even eliminated, if the interviewer pool is very experienced.

The second part of the training is study-specific. That is, prospective interviewers are trained in the administration of the particular questionnaire to be utilized in the upcoming survey. Often, the training session is conducted prior to completion of the final form of the questionnaire. Whenever possible, this time lag should be avoided, but when it is necessary, the training version should be as accurate a replica of the form to be used as possible. On the other hand, some difficulties in wording, instruction clarity, or question sequence can be found and

A. Neutral Role of the Interviewer

Survey research is of necessity based on an unrealistic "stimulus-response" theory of cognition and behavior. It must be assumed that each question will mean the same thing to every respondent, and that every response will mean the same when given by different respondents (Babbie, 1979).

Thus, the interviewer's presence, ideally, should not affect the respondent's perception of a question, nor the kind of answer that is given. The interviewer is a neutral medium through which questions and answers are transmitted. Therefore:

(1) Avoid interjecting your own opinions.
(2) Avoid being "clever."
(3) Avoid any unnecessary or overly enthusiastic reinforcement, such as 'DY-NO-MITE!!"
(4) Be an "active" listener, but only give the minimum of reinforcement, such as "OK," "I see," or therapeutic grunts–"uh-huh."
(5) Never suggest an answer.

B. "Balanced Rapport"

Remember, the telephone interview is still a social interaction situation. You, as interviewer, and the respondent will not only relate to each other according to your respective roles, but also as individuals. Therefore, it is necessary to achieve some kind of "balance" or rapport. That is, a relationship must be established that will not stimulate either incomplete responses or biased responses based on "over-rapport" or an overly "mechanical" interviewing style. Usually the respondent will try to please you and will often give "socially desirable" answers in order to get your reinforcement. This is still true even though you are communicating over the phone and are not physically present to the respondent.

Neutral responses are difficult for most of us, since normal phone behavior finds us trying to convince the other party of something–date, meeting, product to buy, party to go to, etc. We are not neutral, but advocates. Telephone interviewing calls for us to drop this persuasive tactic, except when introducing the interview. It is then and only then that we use our powers of persuasion to get a prospective respondent to agree to an interview.

C. General Tasks of Interviewer

(1) accurate communication of questions;
(2) maximizing the respondent's ability and willingness to answer;
(3) listening actively to determine what is relevant;
(4) *probing* to increase the validity, clarity, and completeness of the response.

D. Specific Tasks

(1) Be familiar with the questionnaire.
(2) Follow question wording and question order exactly; ask *all* of the questions.

FIGURE 5.4   Role of Interviewer

(3) Record responses exactly.
(4) Be casual, conversational, and friendly.
(5) Record first answer; it is usually closer to the truth.
(6) Doublecheck your instructions before you begin.
(7) Repeat answers for respondent if there is any doubt.
(8) Doublecheck questionnaire to be sure that all items have been answered, answers recorded correctly, and status information (phone number, location) completed.

E. Final Comment

Most people like to talk about themselves and what they know. Once their initial anxieties are relieved, the respondent will talk because of this fact and the guarantee of a good listener—you.

FIGURE 5.4 Continued

corrected in interviewer training, before the actual survey commences. In a sense, then, the training session can be a pretest.

This phase may require more than one session. It is not recommended that any training session last longer than two and one-half or three hours in order to avoid fatigue and any possible loss of information due to inattentiveness. Once all questions about the nature and purpose of the study have been discussed, the project director or training supervisor will go over the questionnaire item by item with the interviewers. For each item, response recording instructions, reading guidelines, and potential difficulties are discussed. It is at this time that instructions for branching or filters are elaborated. Survey supervisors should make every effort to anticipate questions that a respondent might ask, such as: "How did you get my number?" or "Who is sponsoring this survey?" and prepare a list of standardized responses for interviewers' use. Figure 5.6 shows a form used in one of the telephone studies conducted under the auspices of the Telephone Survey Center at the University of Nevada, Las Vegas.

Once the item-by-item analysis is completed, each interviewer is then asked to administer the instrument to another person present. Those who play the respondent role can be asked to be "difficult" or "compliant" in their response patterns. During this practice phase, it is productive to stop the interviewing

A. INTRODUCTION

Past research indicates that telephone interviews are seldom terminated once started. However, if a refusal is to occur, it will be between the introductory message and the first question.

Therefore, it is crucial that you state clearly *who you are, who you represent,* and *why you are calling.* Respondents need to feel that their opinions are important and necessary for the survey to be valid. If they hesitate, even after the introduction, you may have to do some *prodding:*

"This won't take much time and we really do want your opinion."

"Since your number was drawn, we need to talk to you in order for our survey to be valid, a true representation of the community."

"Let me remind you that your responses will be confidential."

B. WHOM TO INTERVIEW

(1) We are seeking the opinion of adult members of households, age 18 and over.

(2) You may talk to either males or females. As the study progresses, you will be told whether to concentrate on interviewing more males than females, or vice versa. This will depend on what proportions of the total sample are male and female.

(3) Try to interview the person who answers the phone. If he or she is unable or unwilling to cooperate, try to get another adult member of that household.

(4) If no one will talk at this time, try to establish a time that will be convenient for a call-back (we are not limited to early evening hours—staff are available to call during the day).

(5) A supervisor is available to assist you if you need help in convincing a perspective respondent to continue the interview.

C. HOW MUCH INFORMATION TO GIVE

(1) Read questions precisely, as written.

(2) I repeat, read them precisely as written. It is extremely important that everyone be asked the same question in the same way. Even a difference in one word could drastically change the meaning and, thus, the response.

(3) Information that you can provide to the respondent is listed below (or on attached sheet). Do not go beyond this information to interpret questions from the respondent. Key phrases you might use to answer questions are:

"This is all the information available to us."

"We would like you to answer the question in terms of the way it is stated. Could I read it again for you?"

"I'm sorry I don't have that information."

FIGURE 5.5   Interviewing Guidelines

"I will write on the questionnaire the qualifications to your answer you have just mentioned."

(4) If the respondent still requires more information, call on the operations supervisor for assistance.

D. PROBING

(1) If no open-ended questions are included in the interview schedule, probing for better clarity or for additional information is not necessary.

(2) However, if a respondent is reluctant to answer a question, you may have to *coax* him to answer with statements like:

"Is there anything else you would like to say?"

"Are you sure that is all?"

"Could you elaborate on . . .?"

(3) Be careful about *leading* the respondent. Probes are to be *neutral* requests for information.

(4) If unsure of respondent's final response, repeat what you think it was so that he can confirm or correct it.

E. WHOSE OPINION TO ACCEPT

Everything should be in terms of what the RESPONDENT thinks—not the respondent's kids, friends, boss, bartender, etc. Therefore, you might need to say:

"I see. Now, is that what you think?"

"It's *your* opinion that we really want."

ALSO, DON'T GIVE RESPONDENT *YOUR* OPINION.

F. RECORD EVERY CALL YOU MAKE, even though the number was not working, no answer was received, or the interview was not completed.

(1) You will be provided with numbers to call on a separate sheet. *Do not call any other numbers.*

(2) Please record any pertinent comments on the cover of the questionnaire or in the margins.

G. Do not smoke, eat, or drink coffee, tea, or milk, etc. while conducting the interview. You have too much to concentrate on without having to worry about dropping an ash or spilling a drink onto inappropriate (and perhaps painful) places.

FIGURE 5.5   Continued

H. IF BY CHANCE A PERSON BECOMES INCENSED, USES FOUL LANGUAGE, GOES ON A TIRADE, ETC.

   (1) Be nice! Do not hang up.

   (2) Possible kinds of responses, as situations warrant:

   "Yes, I see." "Uh huh."

   "Yes, I understand you feel quite strongly about this matter, but we really need your opinion."

   "Let me repeat the question for you, sir."

   (3) *Do not,* under any condition, *ARGUE, INSERT YOUR OWN OPINION,* or worst of all, *LOSE YOUR TEMPER.*

   (4) Do not terminate the interview if a respondent is abusive. Only terminate if *subject* refuses to respond.

   If all else fails, wait for the opportunity, and then say something to this effect:

   "I'm awfully sorry you prefer not to complete the interview, but thank you anyway. Goodbye Mr. _____."

I. EXTRANEOUS COMMENTS ABOUT THE QUESTIONS

Insofar as possible, write them down using margins of questionnaire, or the back if necessary.

J. AFTER YOU HANG UP

Go back over every single question and make sure all answers are clearly marked, data on front page are complete, and all written comments are legible. Whenever this is not done, the amount of additional work created gets to be fantastic, and it really slows down the processing. Also, since we usually have to produce the results quickly, we don't want to have to call you at 1:00 a.m. and say: "Now what did you really mean on that call to Alonzio O'Connell in Spring Valley?" Enough said!

K. AFTER EACH SESSION OF INTERVIEWING

   (1) *DO NOT TAKE ANYTHING HOME WITH YOU.* All questionnaires, code sheets, instruction sheets, etc. must be left in the survey center.

   (2) Check out with the supervisor. Confirm the time spent interviewing.

FIGURE 5.5   Continued

L. AFTER YOU HAVE LEFT THE SURVEY CENTER

We are adamant about the following:

The only way we can be successful is to establish and maintain a reputation for confidentiality. Therefore, please:

(1) Do not tell anyone the names or locations of people you interviewed.

(2) Do not tell anyone the substance of any interview or part of an interview, no matter how fascinating or interesting it was. We find it rather disturbing to hear from other faculty members or students details of an interview two weeks after a study is completed. Confidentiality is essential!

(3) Please avoid revealing your summary of findings. Just because 90 percent of your respondents favored small towns doesn't mean 90 percent of everyone else's did too. The problem is that the people you tell will tell others, and they will do the generalizing no matter how good you are at qualifying things.

(4) If people hear about responses of others and then are later called on the same survey, it could influence their responses.

NOTE: The telephone interview is a version of the personal interview, except that you are not engaged in a face-to-face conversation. You have *only* "voice-to-voice" contact to depend on. Therefore, careful attention to these procedures is necessary in order to be sure that you can complete your interview with the right person and get valid information.

FIGURE 5.5 Continued

periodically to receive questions from the interviewers. Often, one interviewer's question may have come to the minds of several others. The variation in difficulty of respondent attitudes gives interviewers practice at persuasion and handling unanticipated questions.

The final training phase is designed to acquaint interviewers with the operational procedures of the survey. They are shown where and how to check in, how to use the phones, how to complete a calling record, and how to edit and file completed questionnaires.

It is crucial that every number called be accounted for. A calling record (Figure 5.7) is maintained for each number, and all calls are coded for status (for example, "complete," "no

1. TELEPHONE RESEARCH FACILITY?

This is a research unit of the College of Arts and Letters of the University of Nevada, Las Vegas, designed for the purpose of conducting public opinion polls on various political, social, and economic issues. The director is Dr. James Frey, Chairman of the Sociology Department. If you have questions or concerns about participating in this study, you may contact him at 739-3322 or 739-3587.

2. WHO IS SPONSORING THIS RESEARCH?

This is a cooperative project of the Sagebrush Alliance and the Department of Sociology of UNLV.

3. WHO, WHAT IS THE SAGEBRUSH ALLIANCE?

The Sagebrush Alliance is a community group concerned with the protection, health, welfare, and safety of this and future generations, particularly in regard to the dangers and potential dangers of radiation.

4. HOW DID YOU GET MY NAME OR NUMBER?

We do not have or need your name. Your number was dialed at random (technique: Random Digit Dialing) without using any list such as the telephone directory.

5. HOW DO I KNOW THIS WILL BE CONFIDENTIAL?

We do not have your name. We are only interested in the combined responses of the nearly 400 people who will be called. No individual's responses will be singled out. All of us that are working on this project are required to follow certain policies and procedures developed for the purpose of protecting everyone's identity.

6. HOW WILL THE RESULTS BE USED?

The information generated by this survey will be utilized by students in research methods classes. In addition, the results will be made available to decision makers in the community to help them understand what the people of Las Vegas think about certain issues as they relate to the use of nuclear power.

7. WHAT IS THE PURPOSE OF THIS SURVEY?

This is a general survey of the public on a number of current issues or problems related to nuclear power. The study is designed to learn how you feel about these matters.

*** DO NOT provide any additional information other than what is included above. If there are questions you cannot answer or if your answer does not satisfy the respondent, call the supervisor.

FIGURE 5.6   Nuclear Power Survey: Questions and Responses
About This Survey

answer," "refusal"). The supervisor can then keep a continuing record of completion rates for each exchange and substitute or supply additional numbers if necessary. The numbers to be called are affixed to the calling record (or preprogrammed if using a CATI survey) prior to the calling time. This can be a rather tedious task, but it is not as subject to error as would be the case if interviewers were required to select numbers.

Interviewers are also instructed not to allow the phone to ring more than four times. Research and observation (Smead and Wilcox, 1980) have demonstrated that 97 percent of households with someone at home will respond by at least the fourth ring; 99 percent will reach the phone within five rings. This is a cost-effective consideration that reduces the nonproductive time of interviewers.

All nonworking, busy, and "no answer" numbers are to be called a second time in order to verify their status. Interviewers should be able to distinguish between a regular busy signal of 60 beeps per minute and a "fast busy" of 120 beeps, which usually means that all circuits are temporarily overloaded. In both cases, call-backs within one-half hour are required. If a record-a-call or mechanical answering device is reached, the interviewer should leave his or her name and the reason for the call. However, it is a rare occasion where the owner of a recording machine—a device often employed to filter out undesired calls—will return a call to the survey center. Very often, these are the most difficult persons to reach, and upward of 12-15 call-backs at various times are necessary to reach answering machine owners or answering service subscribers.

SCHEDULING INTERVIEWS

When making the decision on when to conduct the interviews, the survey director must first be certain that the centralized facility is available for the days on which calls are to be made. Second, when scheduling interviews on those days, the project director should try to have the most interviewers available at times when the probability of nonresponse is small and

Key: Status of Interview

IC - Interview complete
PIC - Partially complete
REF - Refusal
DISC - Disconnect
NA - No answer
BUS - Business phone

Phone Exchange Prefix _____

Calls Made

RANDOM NUMBER	1st Date/Time/Interviewer	2nd Date/Time/Interviewer	3rd Date/Time/Interviewer	INTERVIEW COMPLETION					
				BUS	DISC	NA	REF	PIC	IC

COMMENT

COMMENT

COMMENT

COMMENT

COMMENT

COMMENT

COMMENT

COMMENT

COMMENT

COMMENT

FIGURE 5.7 Interviewer Calling Record

the likelihood of completion great. Most evidence shows that weekday evenings from 5:30 to 9:00 p.m. (Weeks et al., 1980; Vigderhous, 1981) are best. Within that three-and-one-half-hour time block, the hour from 6:00-7:00 p.m. ranks the highest for potential completions. We have discovered this to be true even in Las Vegas, which is a "24-hour" community with three full work shifts. Saturday from 9:00 a.m.-2:00 p.m. and Sunday evenings rank as the next best calling times, followed by weekday hours and holidays (Wiseman and McDonald, 1979). In order to be cost effective, most project directors assign interviewers based on projected completion rates. Thus, fewer interviewers are needed for daytime hours than for the peak evening hours. As the study proceeds, variations are made in the size of the interviewing group. Fewer interviewers are needed as the study draws nearer to its completion. A project director would thus be wise to keep his most productive people working the longest.

Some variations in scheduling occur because of population characteristics. The calling times mentioned above have proved to be most productive for heterogeneous populations like the general public. If the population being surveyed is a specialized group, however, such as professional or business persons, the peak calling times could be the daytime hours, when these prospective respondents can be reached at an office number. Similarly, it would be very difficult to contact a minister at night or a teacher during the day. Thus, before any decisions on scheduling interviews are made, considerable thought must be given to the characteristics of a population and the availability of its members.

There is some evidence of seasonal variations in productive calling. In the most complete analysis available, Vigderhous (1981) discovered that January, February, March, and April were the best months in which to call. June, July, and August were not desirable, since many potential respondents are enjoying vacations and/or other activities outside the home. By far the worst month for conducting surveys is December, because of the holidays and the high demand for everyone's time and attention in the form of school programs, social events, shopping, and religious festivities. Even if people are at home during the summer months and the holiday season, they are more likely to refuse the interview because of other pressing commitments.

Finally, interviewing schedules have to adjust to special events and/or unexpected occurrences. We have already seen why holidays are to be avoided. In addition, our response rate goes down considerably, particularly with males, on Monday nights in the fall of the year. Friday nights are not very productive either, particularly in smaller, rural communities where school and church events often occur in the evening. Even the weather can have an effect on scheduling. Normally, we have only three or four interviewers working on a Friday night at the Telephone Survey Center. However, during one particular statewide survey being conducted in the late fall, the northern (rural) counties of the state were experiencing a very heavy early winter snowfall. Anticipating that this might keep many rural Nevadans at home on Friday, we scheduled a full crew of interviewers. Sure enough, we experienced a higher-than-usual completion rate for those counties on this evening.

Interviewers also need to be scheduled for call-back appointments or to try "no answers" at different times. It is very important to have an interviewer available to call a respondent at the time that he or she has designated. With CATI, this is usually no problem, since the computer will bring up the number at the prescribed time to any interviewer who is currently on line. Keeping track of call-backs is more difficult for paper-and-pencil surveys, since these times must be controlled and assigned manually. A full crew of interviewers need not be assigned to appointed call-backs, since there are usually not enough to keep them busy.

Population characteristics, seasonal variations, the occurrence of special events, the availability of the telephone facility, and hourly and day-of-the-week variations all have an impact on the scheduling of interviews. The primary motivating factor in any decision on scheduling, however, is how best to use the most interviewers, particularly those who are most productive, at the times when they are most likely to achieve high completion rates with few nonresponses, in the form of either refusals or no answers.

Coding and Data Analysis

As indicated earlier, no item in the questionnaire is included without first being reviewed by the people who will be coding the responses for data analysis. This review will identify those coding difficulties, such as open-ended questions, that will ultimately require the construction of categories of responses. It will also identify items where precoding is possible and will assure that any standard use of enumeration is followed throughout the instrument (for example, "Don't know" is always 9 or 99). Thus the coder ensures that the responses will be in a form that makes their transfer to machine-readable symbols efficient.

Coding commences at the same time as interviewing. In order for this to be the case, two tasks must be performed. First, all questionnaires must be edited for completeness and accurate recording of answers. This can be done by a supervisor, but it can also be done by an editor/coder hired specifically for the task. If errors are discovered, the editor obtains immediate clarification from the interviewer and, if necessary, the respondent is called back to obtain a response to an overlooked item or to verify a response.

Second, the code book must be prepared and be ready at the same time as the questionnaire. The code book includes the question number, a brief synopsis of the question, the answer categories, the values assigned to these answer categories, and any variable identification information that is necessary for adaptation to a specific computer program such as the Statistical Program for the Social Sciences (SPSS). If batch processing is used, the IBM card and column numbers are also inserted. Table 5.1 displays a code book format used for a musicians'

TABLE 5.1   Code Book

Card Number – 1

Column	Question Number	SPSS Variable Name	Variable Description and Codes
1			Card number
2-4			Identification number
5	1	VO1	Importance of musical ability in getting job
			1. Very important
			2. Somewhat important
			3. Not very important
			8. Refuse to answer
			9. Don't know
6-7	2	VO2	Musical instrument played
			01. Trumpet
			02. Trombone
			03. Saxaphone
			.
			.
			.
			88. Refuse to answer
			99. Don't know
8	3	VO3	Find real enjoyment in job
			1. Strongly agree
			2. Agree
			3. Disagree
			4. Strongly disagree
			8. Refuse to answer
			9. Don't know

survey conducted by the University of Nevada's Survey Center. Note that the SPSS variable names have been designated as numbers only. It is possible to provide more descriptive identifications (for example, "MUSABIL"); however, such assignment is not necessary, as the names can be matched to variable numbers during subsequent phases in the data processing.

In some cases it is not necessary to develop a code book. If precoding on the questionnaire is possible for all items, the data can be transferred directly from the computer to a card or disk without the intermediary use of a summary code sheet or mark sense card. Ordinarily, this is only possible when the questions are of a closed-ended variety or when all possible answer categories can be anticipated. Questionnaires with many open-ended items, or with a significant degree of screening as the result of certain specialized response patterns, can be partially precoded but will also require the guidance of a code book. This reduces the potential for confusion and subsequent coding error.

The existence of preprogrammed computer packages such as SPSS or BASK makes data analysis a less cumbersome task than it was in the past. It is no longer necessary to write unique and elaborate series of program statements to obtain a correlation or any other type of statistic. One only needs to inform the computer that the subprogram "descriptive statistics" or "partial correlation" is desired. This means that the project director and his or her data analysis associates can devote more energy to the determination of the more substantive issues (for example, the effect of one variable on another) of data analysis once the data have been prepared for this phase of the research.

Attention to the details of telephone survey implementation is crucial not only to the administrative success of the survey, but also to data quality. Controlling respondent selection, interviewer error, and coding error through proper supervision and administrative procedure will result in data that are more reliable and trustworthy. The advent of computer usage, centralized facilities, and improved supervisory practices gives the telephone survey a considerable advantage when compared to the face-to-face interview. The latter will always have problems with respondent selection and interviewer error as long as there is dependence on the interviewer to work alone in the field.

Notes

1. The content of this figure is based on my associations with many projects at the Social Research Center of Washington State University and as Director of the Telephone Survey Center at the University of Nevada, Las Vegas. Advice on compiling the figure was provided by Don A. Dillman and his Washington State University staff, and by Carol Hunter of the Nevada facility.

2. These costs include only direct costs such as wages, printing, and the like. Overhead or indirect costs are highly variable among organizations, making it unsafe to provide cost guidelines that include both types of expenditures. The costs noted here are applicable to the 1981-82 experiences of the University of Nevada Telephone Survey Center. Hence, generalization of their application should be done with some caution.

3. AT&T's *Notes on the Network* (1980) provides a detailed description of how Outward WATS and Inward WATS (800 service) work, including the assignment of area boundaries and subscription mechanics.

4. For a more detailed description of CATI technology and procedures, see Shure and Meeker (1978), Fielder (1979), Fink (1981), and Shanks et al. (1981).

5. The Survey Center at Berkeley recently completed an experiment comparing direct data entry (DDE) costs with those of conventional keypunching and coding procedures. They concluded that DDE is both time and cost effective and can reduce coding and cleaning by 25-50 percent (Survey Research, 1981).

6. For more details, contact Harry Sharp, Director of the Wisconsin Survey Research Laboratory in Madison, Wisconsin.

CHAPTER 6

FINAL CONSIDERATIONS AND
THE FUTURE

There can be no doubt that the use of telephone surveys will only increase in the future. While not the favorite of respondents (National Research Council, 1979), telephone surveys, as opposed to those conducted by mail or face-to-face, are likely to be preferred to a greater extent by project directors because of the benefits of lower cost, enhanced data quality, ease of administration, and reduced data retrieval time that can be attributed to telephone surveys. In fact, a market survey official recently predicted that by the early 1980s nearly 75 percent of all survey work will be done by phone (Blankenship, 1977). Although I do not have concrete evidence, I suspect that this prediction is not far from being correct.

The steadily increasing costs of postage and the apparent decline in mail service efficiency, plus the lengthy time frame required for data retrieval, all work against the attractiveness of a mail survey in a cost-conscious, rapidly changing world that demands immediate information feedback at the lowest price. The rising costs in wages and travel, in addition to the continual decline in completion rates for face-to-face surveys, suggest that this form of survey research will also be utilized with less frequency. This method also suffers from the inability to deliver data within a time frame that is acceptable, particularly to policymakers and other clients of research who need up-to-date data input for a pending decision. Finally, the improved data quality that comes as the result of developments in research design and technology will add to the attractiveness of the telephone survey technique.

The previous chapters represent an effort to describe some of the recent developments in sampling, questionnaire design, and administration that are being utilized in association with telephone surveys. Unfortunately, changes and improvements are occurring at a rate that makes even the most recent publication out of date (though not necessarily impractical). The material contained here should be helpful to any researcher who wants to conduct a telephone survey. However, that researcher needs to be aware of new developments, particularly technological, and the procedural and ethical implications of those developments. The remainder of this chapter deals with these issues.

Technological Developments

The major developments in telephone survey technology have taken the form of an interface of the computer with the telephone.[1] Computer-Assisted Telephone Interviewing (CATI), discussed earlier in Chapter 2, represents the most familiar example of recent technological innovation. CATI systems are designed to assist an interviewer with questionnaire administration and to provide a mechanism by which large quantities of data can be accumulated, stored, and manipulated more efficiently than with a paper-and-pencil or manual survey. Improvements in the software for sample selection, questionnaire administration, and data analysis are in the works at the University of California, Berkeley, and other institutions with CATI systems. These systems will be even more attractive once hardware adaptations have been made so that microcomputers can be utilized.

While CATI has developed as an aid to interviewing and data analysis, other developments are occurring that have the ominous potential of eliminating the interviewer altogether. Computerized dialing, screening, and recording are now possible. In fact, many of us have probably been interviewed "by computer" at one time. With the assistance of a computer and a prerecorded message in the form of an introduction and a series of questions, it is possible to dial a number and interview a respondent without the physical presence of an interviewer. The respondent's answers are either recorded by voice or can be sent directly to the computer by simply touching one or a combination of numbers on the phone. Another version of this system is to utilize the computer to dial the number and the recorded message to screen for a particular type of respondent, with a signal (light or buzz) telling the interviewer present to pick up the phone and administer the interview. A recorded message terminates the interview should the respondent not be qualified or decline the interview.

Computerized dialing and recording is faster and less costly than employing a pool of persons to engage in sample selection and interviewing, but this approach is dehumanizing, as few of us like to "talk to computers," and automated dialing may lead to higher than usual refusal rates as a result of this resentment. In addition, there are still problems of locating and programming usable phone numbers, and respondents must have a touch-tone phone to be able to respond.

Mechanical failures of either telephone, recording, or computer equipment could adversely affect sample selection and data storage. This type of system has been put to use with fair results by some newspapers and polling firms conducting "instant polls" requiring responses to only a few questions, but it is difficult to imagine the effective use of this computer-assisted technique with a questionnaire of any length. In order for this system to work, the programmer would have to be able to anticipate all contingencies (that is, all variations in a respondent's answers), in order to be able to obtain the proper recording of responses. Finally, this type of interviewing does not permit clarification or controlled probing; it practically eliminates the effective use of open-ended questions in surveys.

Automated dialing and recording have been utilized more frequently by commercial marketing firms when engaged in sales promotion than by conventional survey firms conducting standard social science surveys. Marketing firms will sometimes use this system to develop sales leads, obtain requests for a salesman to call, gather information about the extent of product use (for example, ceiling insulation) in order to send out a salesman, or to determine if there is interest in a product in a certain marketing area. Very often these solicitations will initiate a conversation with some statement like: "We are conducting a survey," but instead of proceeding as if it were a legitimate survey with a series of neutral questions on the mentioned topic, the caller continues with a sales solicitation. The apparent success of this approach has stimulated new uses of the telephone for purposes other than gathering information or inquiring about one's health. However, with the institutionalization of survey research and the high visibility of this kind of inquiry among the general public, it has been much easier to get a "foot in the door" by introducing the solicitation under the guise of a legitimate survey. As early as the mid-1960s, one report showed that 60 percent of a sample had been approached for an interview that had ended up in a sales solicitation at least once; 52 percent of the sample had had this experience more than once (Biel, 1969). This phenomenon became known as the "phony interview" and has been made easier by virtue of the development of automated dialing and recording.

If people resent phone sales in person, they are many times more resentful if called by a computer. A "Letter to the Editor" in the *Los Angeles Times* depicts one person's feeling:

> The other evening, as I was preparing to make a call, the telephone rang and I answered it. Guess what was calling me. (sic) The recorded message identified itself as XL6000 and proceeded to ask if I wanted to make more on my investments. Then, after a sales pitch for nothing that could be identified, the machine proceeded to ask for my name, address and *telephone number*. While the message was going on, I also tried to break the connection to confirm what my wife had said about her call, I could not get a dial tone until the message was completed.

> I believe that the public should be aware that we are being used in such a program, and should respond against such an invasion of privacy with any action that the people think suitable to discourage the use of such a machine.

Telephone survey research has suffered to some extent, heretofore undocumented, because many potential respondents who were fooled by a phony interview now refuse to agree to any requests for interviews, no matter what the sponsor. We do not as yet know what proportion of refusals can be attributed to experiences with "junk calls," but it is fair to predict that phony interviews do produce some refusals.

In order to protect persons from junk phone calls, the Bell System has developed what is designated as Common Channel Interoffice Signaling (CCIS). This device represents a network that carries the caller's number so that a person will know the origin of the call before picking up the receiver. An "intelligent telephone" hooked into the CCIS would indicate different kinds of calls by different ringing tones, colored lights, or even an electronic readout display of the calling number. The system can also be programmed to screen calls so that some are patched through, others deflected to an answering service, and still others forwarded to another number. Priority calls would flash a green light, and these would be precoded with a special three-digit number known only to a select few callers. This system is an improvement over the answering device, since it not only gives a clue to the identity of callers before actually picking up the phone, but it also allows one to answer the desired calls without delay. A survey researcher may never reach the CCIS subscriber because the survey call stimulates an undesirable message code, and because a random calling schedule will not permit circumvention of the system, as is the case with answering devices. Should this system become available on a reasonable basis to the general public, representative samples might become a phenomenon of the past.

Three additional technological developments have potential use for survey researchers. First, the videophone has been perfected from a technical standpoint but is not available on a general basis. If used in telephone research, it could make the telephone interview much like that of the face-to-face setting. This would mean that nonverbal cues and visual aids could be meaningfully incorporated into telephone data gathering. The cost of this device is its major obstacle to generalized use. The second device is more of a program than a unique technological innovation. The expanded availability of personalized CRT installations in homes and offices has opened up the possibility of "Computerized Conferencing" (Hiltz and Turoff, 1978). Through networks such as TELENET, ARPANET, and CON-FER, people in disparate and dispersed settings can communicate via computer hook-up. While this system has experienced limited use in "telephonic delphi" decision making or conferencing, it does have potential applicability to survey research, particularly if the relevant population has access to a CRT terminal.[2] In this case, all questions and answers would appear on a screen before respondent or interviewer (that is, the key operator), and no voice messages would transpire. Under this system, no interviewer would be required.

Third, it is now possible to foresee the eventual computerization of all interview situations. For example, surveys can now be conducted via television with the respondent simply dialing (touching) certain numbers on a device that transmits the responses directly to a central computer. The results are almost instantaneously displayed on the screen. A prime example of this type of information technology is Warner Amex Cable Communications' QUBE, which is a *two-way television* interactive system. Advocates of interactive television assert that QUBE and systems like it enhance democracy by promoting civic exchanges (Elshtain, 1982: 108). Opponents maintain that such systems establish instant plebiscites and encourage authoritarian rule of the views of the majority, where there would be no need for debate, only a calculation of opinion. From a survey research standpoint, one cannot be sure how the QUBE results were tabulated, how many persons responded, and how representative these respondents were. It is highly likely, for example, that children could respond to questions that required adult experience or knowledge. The Standards Committee of the American Association of Public Opinion Research is currently investigating the potential practical and ethical impacts of the "robotics" of opinion polling—"the transformation of method and substance wrought by technology" (Gollin, 1982: 5).

Except for the CATI systems, the technological developments described above have not been used by most survey researchers, although these same pollsters have become quite concerned about the implications of this technology, particularly the interactive television systems. One very real concern, beyond those of political manipulation and privacy invasion, is that of proliferating these types of "instant polls" to the point that their accuracy is meaningless. There is enough difficulty obtaining valid data under normal survey conditions; trying to obtain it under "speed-up" conditions is nearly impossible. As the public becomes more aware of polls and their flaws, the more likely that all surveys will lose credibility. Calls are now being made to curtail the enthusiasm of the new pollsters (for example, on television) and to proceed at a moderate, more productive pace (Gollin, 1980).

Ethical Issues: Need to Know Versus Right to Know

There has always been concern that social scientists respect the rights of participants in research, regardless of the type of inquiry. But in recent years, perhaps as a result of such celebrated instances as the Milgram experiments or the "Invisible Ink" caper,[3] even greater attention has been directed at protecting the rights of respondents. Issues of confidentiality, privacy, and informed consent have been given prominent safeguards in professional codes of ethics, grant-giving agency regulations, and federal law.

CODE OF ETHICS

Every discipline has a code of ethics similar to those of the National Council on Polls and the American Association for Public Opinion Research (AAPOR) (see Appendix A). Reynolds (1979) has reviewed 24 codes selected for social science research and has put together a composite code of 78 items covering the topics of informed consent, anonymity, and the reporting of results. Tremblay and Dillman (1977: 74) have also reviewed several codes and found the following five themes:

(1) The researcher must always strive to protect the confidentiality of information obtained from respondents and their identity.
(2) Participation in research by a respondent must be voluntary.
(3) Research should infringe on the respondent's privacy to as little degree as possible.
(4) Respondents must be protected from any harm that could result from the study.
(5) The purpose and sponsor of the research must be identified to the respondent. Deceit should not be used.

Despite these principles, which would be agreeable to most social scientists, there is still the personal ethics of the researcher to consider. Some would adhere strictly to the code; others may not be so compliant. Correcting for this variance would require a mechanism of supervision and sanction that any professional body would reluctantly implement for reasons of colleagueship and autonomy. Only in the most spectacular instances would any effort at sanction be tried, and then with reticence. For example, even though considerable abuse of these principles has occurred, particularly with the use of deceit via phony surveys or junk calls, little or nothing has been done by survey groups or legislators to curb these abuses.

INFORMED CONSENT

Administrative regulations and federal law have specified the parameters of the legal dimensions of informed consent, privacy, and confidentiality. The U.S. Department of Health and Human Services guidelines governing research supported under its grants requires that a signed consent form be completed if research participants are "at risk" (DHEW, 1971). No informed consent policy is designed to prevent social science research, particularly where some risk is involved, but it does require that respondents be informed (Nachmias and Nachmias, 1981). Risk includes such obvious items as exposure to pain or any effort that could result in either injury or other forms of physical discomfort. Also included under the umbrella of risk are invasion of privacy and psychological stress, items more applicable to survey research than pain and physical suffering. It is possible that sensitive or probing attitude survey questions could create psychological or emotional stress on the part of the respondent. Certainly, revelations on many items, including the demographic, can be interpreted as invasions of privacy. This potential exists in any survey, and therefore informed consent must be implemented.

Federal government criteria for informed consent include "what a reasonable and prudent person would want to know." The required elements include:

(1) a fair explanation of the procedures to be followed and their purposes;
(2) a description of the attendant discomforts and risks reasonably to be expected;
(3) a description of benefits reasonably to be expected;
(4) a disclosure of appropriate alternative procedures that might be advantageous to the participant;
(5) an offer to answer any inquiries concerning the procedure;
(6) an instruction that the person is free to withdraw his or her consent and to discontinue participation in the project at any time without prejudice to the participant [DHEW, 1971: 7].

The most controversial of these structures is the first, for there is a continuous debate, as yet unsettled, over how much information to provide a respondent in advance. Too much information could invalidate the results, and too little could create suspicion and a refusal to participate. It is often difficult to describe risks and discomforts, since these could require an overly technical explanation. It is also not possible to predict, in surveys, if a respondent will feel psychological or emotional stress in answering some questions. The guarantee of confidentiality, however, may go a long way to ease the respondent's anxiety about participating.

In telephone surveys, it is virtually impossible to obtain a signed informed consent unless such a form is mailed with a preletter, or if a request to send such a form is made during the interview. Neither is usually done, and the latter is particularly a problem for the guarantee of anonymity. As a result, telephone survey researchers can only assume that the respondent is a responsible, mature individual who, given the relevant information, can make an informed decision. Thus, the introduction will usually contain a statement such as: "May I proceed?" or something as cryptic as "Okay?" This gives the respondent the opportunity, once he has heard the introduction—including the purpose, sponsor, relevant sampling information, and disclaimers of confidentiality and rights to terminate—to decide to continue or to refuse to be interviewed. Once the interview proceeds, the respondent can terminate quite easily, although there is evidence that the norms of telephone behavior suggest that the caller must terminate the conversation; compliance to this norm can "force" the respondent to continue. In a sense, then, respondents may lose their autonomy or a component of privacy because they are not free to make the decision to participate on their own terms. This needs further research elaboration. However, few critics would question an introduction that does, in fact, ask for the respondent's permission to continue.

CONFIDENTIALITY

Provisions to protect the confidentiality of a respondent's answers and identity are required by the "Protection of Human Subjects" guidelines of the Code of Federal Regulations. Confidentiality refers to the safeguarding of any information about one person which is known by another. Thus, the interviewer must not share this information or in any way link responses to specific providers. If he or she were to do so, a respondent could be identified; if the responses are anonymous, identification is not possible. Unfortunately, the latter is virtually impossible to achieve, since having a number and a completed questionnaire can usually lead one to a respondent's identity.

In reality, it is difficult to know whether or not a respondent believes the guarantees of confidentiality provided by the researcher. The National Research Council (1979) demonstrated by means of experimental variations in confidentiality assurances that promises of confidentiality or the lack of it were not a factor in determining response or nonresponse. Many refusals occurred before the confidentiality statement. However, once past the introduction, which included a variation of the confidentiality statement, there was an association between the degree to which confidentiality was assured and refusals. The study also showed that most respondents were skeptical of surveys, as 50 percent indicated that surveys could be trusted some of the time, but not always. Another study indicated that confidentiality was important to response, but that if over-emphasized, it could increase respondent apprehension and negatively affect data (Reamer, 1979). Thus, some persons will refuse to participate even before the confidentiality statement is read, and many of these refusals will be the result of a lack of trust, though once into the introduction, a simple declarative statement: "Your answers will be confidential," may be all that is needed to satisfy legal scrutiny and respondent concern.

Surveys in Court. The issue of whether survey researchers' guarantee of confidentiality will hold up to a court subpoena is one that will probably be of considerable concern as the frequency and diversity of telephone surveys increase. So far, academicians and survey researchers have not been able to obtain the same "shield law" protection as have newspaper reporters. However, two recent court cases suggest that scholars will receive the protection of the court when it comes to revealing respondents' identities, should their data be subpoenaed for a civil court case. In 1972, Samuel Popkin of Harvard went to jail rather than reveal sources of information on Vietnam and the Pentagon Papers to a grand jury (Carroll,

1973). This was the first case in American law where this issue presented itself. It was not tested further by appeal, as Popkin was released when the grand jury was discharged. More recently, a California federal judge ruled: "A scholar does not have to disclose confidential information gathered during his research, even if it might affect the outcome of a civil suit" in denying a utility company the right to information on sources from two Harvard researchers who had just completed interviewing employees of the company (Nejelski, 1976). In both of the cases cited above, the researchers were engaged in basic research that did not involve telephone surveys.

It is difficult to say what the outcome would be if survey data were to be used in court, say, to support a change-of-venue request, in which case the court would want the names of the respondents in order to counteract any hearsay arguments. If the researcher had made the effort to remove all identifiers (for example, telephone numbers, street addresses, names) from each questionnaire and had verified each interview with his or her signature along with the interviewer's, then there should be no problem with hearsay. In any case, it is always a good idea to separate identifying information from the questionnaire as soon as it has been verified and coded.

Perhaps the crucial factor to response is not the guarantee of confidentiality, but the feelings a respondent has toward survey research. If he or she feels the survey to be a legitimate enterprise and his participation justified, the person will be interviewed no matter what the extent of the confidentiality guarantee. Still, respondents need to feel that conditions of trust do exist and that they need not fear any recrimination from their responses. Despite some general skepticism, this climate of trust can be established if the fraternity of survey researchers, individually and collectively, does all that it can to protect the rights of respondents.

Since most research shows a favorable impression of survey research among the general population (Blankenship, 1977; National Research Council, 1979), it can be expected that the trust level for surveys is somewhat high. If researchers do not mistreat respondents with deceit (for example, lying about goals or interview length), with unusually forceful persuasion by an interviewer, or with unnecessary invasion of privacy with sensitive questions (for example, about income, religion, social views) without first establishing rapport and credibility, then this trust should continue to result in fairly high response rates.

The confidentiality of survey data and respondents' identification may be tested in the courtroom in a rather dramatic fashion sooner than we realize, because there has been a definite increase in the use of survey data in the courtroom and other legal settings (Dutka, 1980). Public opinion surveys are admissible evidence that can be used by either side in a court case as part of their evidentiary presentations or as part of the pretrial preparations. The earliest use of survey data occurred in cases where public recognition of a trade symbol was at issue (Cannito and Becker, 1979). Later, with mixed success, survey data were utilized to support a motion for a change of venue. Judges have been reluctant to admit survey data as evidence for these motions, preferring to demand that the defendant prove prejudice in the community. The greatest use today is found with business firms that incorporate survey findings in their appearances before regulatory commissions and other courts. The weight of consumer opinion, in these cases, is a legal aid (Dutka, 1980). Trademark infringement cases, misleading advertising allegations, utility rate petitions, Internal Revenue Service appeals, and arbitration hearings have been defended or appealed with survey data. This trend to use survey data in court has important implications for the conduct of surveys and the actions of researchers.

When survey data are utilized in the judicial process, careful attention must be paid to the methodological procedure and sampling, since the courts are suspicious of a survey commissioned by one side or the other. The survey researcher who is hired by a law firm must be even more careful that the questions he/she asks are not geared to the desired result, and that the sample is representative of the population in question. In some cases, survey data have been ruled inadmissible because the law firm client had a hand in the questionnaire design. All work must be documented because it will be subject to severe scrutiny by the opponent. Interviewers should have no knowledge of the client's identity or the purpose of the study (Dutka, 1980). These individuals could be called to testify on the field execution. Finally, the interviewer and the field supervisor should sign off on each interview in order to verify the fact that it was, in fact, conducted in the time period specified in the affidavit the project director will most certainly have to prepare. It must be clear that data-gathering procedures were well within traditional survey practices in areas such as sample selection and questionnaire design. This will be particularly crucial for the use of telephone surveys, since they may not be defined as traditional in the same sense that the face-to-face interview has been, although new developments in telephone survey administration, particularly CATI, which enhance quality control of the survey, have made telephone survey data more acceptable to courtroom standards.

When survey data are used in judiciary hearings, they are subject to careful scrutiny, and the project director will most certainly be subject to verbal aggression from lawyers and to critical evaluation from a fellow researcher employed as an expert witness by the other side. Thus, not only are the data on trial, so are the credentials of the survey researcher or the person chiefly responsible for the design and supervision of the survey in question. In these cases, the skills of the researcher, not his or her substantive knowledge, are more relevant, since the researcher has been employed as a technician, not a theorist, by the law firm/client (Buffington, 1980). As the project director, or as an expert witness evaluating a colleague's work, the survey researcher must be prepared to handle probing cross-examination on the survey's design and execution, its statistical validity, and its objectivity. Comments by the researcher on the relation of the results to the issue in question should be avoided and left to the lawyers.

The increasing appearance of survey researchers as expert witnesses is consistent with the recent trend of permitting social scientists, including sociologists, psychologists, economists, to testify as experts. While the results of this tendency have not been ascertained, it is possible that frequent court appearances could be detrimental to the survey profession, as they have been for psychiatry, or they could enhance the status and credibility of applied survey research; we will have to wait for that verdict.

Future Research

Recent technological developments, plus improvements in the design and execution of telephone surveys, have provided considerable impetus to the establishment of the telephone survey as an acceptable data-gathering technique in the academic, commercial, and public policy communities. But there is considerable work that remains to be done.

Response quality, as it is reflected in refusals, item nonresponse, and answer completeness, needs further investigation. Variations in study design, introductory statements, topic, interview length, and interviewer behavior need to be tested for their impact on response quality (Groves and Kahn, 1979; Dillman, 1978). In addition, we need to know more about the effects of various pacing rates, variations in income questions, question order, and item complexity on response patterns.

We also do not have much information on the impact of respondent burden or the difficulty, perceived or objective, of responding to a telephone questionnaire. Ordinarily, this burden is defined in terms of demand in time (Sharp and Frankel, 1981), but it can also be articulated as a subjective phenomenon or the manner in which the task of completion is perceived by the respondent. In a Bureau of Social Science Research study utilizing the factors of time demand, recall, and repeat administration, Bradburn (1977) found no differences in response patterns and a generally positive view of surveys. This suggests that respondent burden may not be as significant a problem as originally thought. However, the exact role of the perception of burden in referrals has yet to be determined.

Investigation also needs to be made into the real impact of "phony" or "junk" calls—particularly those conducted with the assistance of automated dialing systems—on response rates in general. We are suspicious that many potential respondents are refusing to participate in these surveys and exercising the termination even before the interviewer can make the introductory statement.

Finally, there is one type of interviewing that has rarely been utilized by telephone researchers but which has some possibilities in specialized instances. That form is the group interview. Market researchers have utilized the group or "focus group" interview for years in their efforts at product evaluation. The ability to arrange for a conferencelike setting through conference call telephone technology makes it possible to conduct a telephone interview with several persons at one time. Blankenship and Pearson (1977) utilized this technique in a market survey and found it less costly than bringing the group together at one setting, advantageous because the telephone company bears the brunt of making the arrangements, and because respondents can participate without leaving the more comfortable confines of office or home. Problems similar to a conventional telephone survey remain, however, such as the inability to use visuals or to read nonverbal cues. This technique cannot be effectively utilized for general public surveys, except perhaps in the early phases of questionnaire development, but it might have significant applicability with elite, very specialized groups or in situations where the sampling unit is a group, not an individual. Still being developed is a more sophisticated version of this technique, one that substitutes a CRT terminal for the speakerphone (Hiltz and Turoff, 1978). Again, its utilization is restricted to specialized populations, or at least to those with access to a CRT.

Concluding Remarks

Telephone survey research has come a long way in popularity and in technological/administrative sophistication since it began to be used with some consistency by academic and commercial researchers in the early 1950s. Its use will only increase in the face of demands for reliable and immediately available data from the diverse clients of this kind of research. While we favor the increased use of telephone surveys, we hope with Dillman (1978) that "survey mania" does not take place, where everyone wants to conduct a survey even for the most trivial of questions. We have not reached the point where the public feels overburdened by the number of requests for surveys, but greater resistance to participation could be the result if some caution is not taken with respect to the appropriate use of the telephone survey. It may also be that the necessity of surveying larger and larger samples, plus the need for nearly impeccable execution, as demanded in forensic surveys, will favor larger survey firms, those more likely to have computer-assisted interviewing systems and other resources that make data gathering more cost effective, as well as producing information of a higher quality.

Finally, there is the danger that the increased use of surveys, particularly telephone surveys, the widespread publication of the results of this usage, and multiple participation by individuals (no longer prevented by random selection) will create a phenomenon that might be designated as the "institutionalization" of the respondent role. That is, by constant exposure to the interview situation, it is possible to learn the expectations, norms, and other factors that make up the social context of the interview. The result is similar to playing any role; we react in terms of sociostructural considerations and not in terms of our authentic feelings or behavior. The social construction of reality might be such that a respondent knows that he or she is part of a sample and therefore should speak as a "representative" of the group being sampled. Since every study has a purpose, the respondent may answer in terms of that goal, thereby eliciting favored responses. If enough persons are able to assume the "postural" position of respondent, rather than a more spontaneous stance, there may be a reverse regression effect and the actual variations or randomization of behavior, values, attitudes,

or beliefs will not be enumerated by the survey. This routinization of the respondent role also has the function of privacy
protection, since responses are made by role expectations, not
actual feelings. This effect may mean that survey organizations
will have to expend greater efforts monitoring the frequency
and use of surveys, as well as doing more research on their
impact on the public.

Notes

1. Survey researchers wishing to monitor developments in telephone technology
and regulations can consult three publications:

Telephony   *Business Communications Review*
Telephone Publishing Corp.   BCR Enterprises
55 E. Jackson   950 York Road
Chicago, IL 60604   Hinsdale, IL 60521
Weekly, $32 subscription fee   Bimonthly, $66 annual subscription

Telephone: Engineer and Management
Harcourt Brace Jovanovich
124 South 1st St.
Geneva, IL 60134
Biweekly, $25 annual subscription

2. AT&T recently opened two teleconferencing centers in New York City and
Washington, DC. They plan to have over forty such centers by the end of 1982. A
one-hour session hooking east and west coast participants will cost approximately
$2,000 per hour. A firm can install its own equipment for about $230,000 plus a
monthly rental fee.

3. See Dickson et al. (1977) for a discussion of the implications of discovering
that the identity of a respondent has been matched to a questionnaire by clandestine
means (for example, by using invisible ink).

APPENDIX A
National Council on Public Polls

Principles of Disclosure

We, the member organizations of the National Council on Public Polls, hereby affirm our commitment to standards of disclosure designed to insure that consumers of survey results that enter the public domain have an adequate basis for judging the reliability and validity of the results reported.

It shall not be the purpose of this Code to pass judgment on the merits of methods employed in specific surveys. Rather, it shall be our sole purpose to insure that pertinent information is disclosed concerning methods that were used so that consumers of surveys may assess studies for themselves.

Any survey organization, upon providing evidence to the Council of its compliance with this Code, shall be permitted to state that it "complies with the Principles of Disclosure of the National Council on Public Polls."

To the above ends, we agree with the following Principles of Disclosure and procedures to be followed in the event question is raised about compliance with them.

PRINCIPLES

All reports of survey findings of member organizations, prepared specifically for public release, will include reference to the following:

— sponsorship of the survey;
— dates of interviewing;
— method of obtaining the interviews (in-person, telephone, or mail);
— population that was sampled;

- size of the sample;
- size and description of the subsample, if the survey report relies primarily on less than the total sample;
- complete wording of questions upon which the release is based; and
- the percentages upon which conclusions are based.

When survey results are released to any medium by a survey organization, the above items will be included in the release and a copy of the release will be filed with the Council within two weeks.

Survey organizations reporting results will endeavor to have print and broadcast media include the above items in their news stories and make a report containing these items available to the public upon request.

Organizations conducting privately commissioned surveys should make clear to their clients that the client has the right to maintain the confidentiality of survey findings. However, in the event the results of a privately commissioned poll are made public by the survey organization, it shall be assumed that they have entered the public domain and the above eight items should be disclosed. In the event the results of a privately commissioned poll are made public by the client and the client acknowledges the release, the survey organization (a) shall make the information outlined above available to the public upon request; and (b) shall have the responsibility to release the information above and other pertinent information necessary to put the client's release into the proper context if such a release has misrepresented the survey's findings.

PROCEDURE

It is reasonable to require disclosure of pertinent information regarding methods when questions are raised about survey results or how a survey has been conducted. The purpose of such disclosure will be to insure that adequate information is available, not to evaluate the specific techniques that were employed.

Accordingly, the procedures outlined below will be used when question is raised:

(a) whether a member organization has complied with the Principles of Disclosure; or
(b) regarding the methods employed in a survey by a member organization and the complaining party has not been able to obtain the desired information directly.

These procedures are designed to insure due process:

1. The President will make available a copy of the complaint to the member organization involved, including the identity of the individual or organization bringing the complaint.

2. The Committee on Disclosure will consider the matter and determine whether or not the question is of sufficient significance to warrant fuller disclosure of methods employed.

3. If two-thirds of a quorum of the Committee feel the question is sufficiently important, the matter will be pursued as described below. Otherwise, the matter will be dropped.

(a) The Committee on Disclosure will determine (by two-thirds vote of a quorum) within one month which aspects of methodology shall be required to be disclosed, including, but not limited to, any or all of the following:

- sample design: sampling frame, stages, number of sampling points, clustering, respondent selection, number of callbacks, refusal rate, substitution rules (if any), and noncontact rate of sample units;

- sample composition: weighted and unweighted demographics for the sample upon which reported results are based (including nonsamples if reports are based upon less than the total sample);

- questions preceding the question or questions upon which reported results are based that may bias the pattern of response;

- all filter questions that were used when results of a partial sample are reported;

- weighting procedures which bear upon the derivation of reported results; and

- sampling error.

(b) Within two weeks of a decision by the Committee on Disclosure, the member organization will be notified by the Chairman of the Committee about which methodological aspects the Committee feels information should be disclosed.

(c) The member organization shall then have two weeks to make the information available to the Committee on Disclosure without prejudice or to indicate why it feels it cannot provide the requested information.

(d) In the event the member organization does not provide the requested information to the Committee on Disclosure within the two-week period, the Chairman will report to the President of the

Council, who will in turn advise the full Council of the impasse by presenting (a) the question raised initially, (b) the request for information of the Committee on Disclosure, and (c) the reply of the member organization.

(e) The matter will then be put to a vote of the full Council, which can by majority vote decide that the member organization can be placed on probation for a specified period of time or even expelled from the Council. In either case, the member organization shall be precluded from stating that its surveys comply with the Principles of Disclosure of the Council, unless and until it is restored to good standing.

(f) In the event the Committee on Disclosure determines that the question raised is significant enough to proceed as outlined in this protocol, the record of the actions of the Committee and the response of the member organizations shall be made public through publication in a relevant publication.

(g) In the event that a party to a disagreement feels due process has not been followed, two courses of action may be taken: (a) the entire matter shall be turned over to the American Arbitration Association and all parties agree that its determination shall be binding, including its allocation of any expenses that may be incurred; or (b) the entire matter shall be discussed at a hearing called for the purposes of informing the organization why sanctions have been recommended and giving the organization the opportunity to defend its position of noncompliance to the membership of the Council with a complete record of such hearing kept and made available to the public upon request.

APPENDIX B
American Association for
Public Opinion Research

Code of Professional Ethics and Practices

We, the members of the American Association for Public Opinion Research, subscribe to the principles expressed in the following code. Our goal is to support sound practice in the profession of public opinion research. (By public opinion research we mean studies in which the principal source of information about individual beliefs, preferences, and behavior is a report given by the individual himself.)

We pledge ourselves to maintain high standards of scientific competence and integrity in our work, and in our relations with our clients and with the general public. We further pledge ourselves to reject all tasks or assignments which would be inconsistent with the principles of this code.

The Code

I. Principles of Professional Practice in the Conduct of Our Work

A. We shall exercise due care in gathering and processing data, taking all reasonable steps to assure the accuracy of results.

B. We shall exercise due care in the development of research designs and in the analysis of data.

(1) We shall employ only research tools and methods of analysis which, in our professional judgment, are well suited to the research problem at hand.
(2) We shall not select research tools and methods of analysis because of their special capacity to yield a desired conclusion.
(3) We shall not knowingly make interpretations of research results, nor shall we tacitly permit interpretations which are inconsistent with the data available.

---

(4) We shall not knowingly imply that interpretations should be accorded greater confidence than the data actually warrant.

C. We shall describe our findings and methods accurately and in appropriate detail in all research reports.

II. Principles of Professional Responsibility in Our Dealings with People

A. The Public:

(1) We shall cooperate with legally authorized representatives of the public by describing the methods used in our studies.
(2) We shall maintain the right to approve the release of our findings, whether or not ascribed to us. When misinterpretation appears, we shall publicly disclose what is required to correct it, notwithstanding our obligation for client confidentiality in all other respects.

B. Clients or Sponsors:

(1) We shall hold confidential all information obtained about the client's general business affairs and about the findings of research conducted for the client, except when the dissemination of such information is expressly authorized.
(2) We shall be mindful of the limitations of our techniques and facilities and shall accept only those research assignments which can be accomplished within these limitations.

C. The Profession:

(1) We shall not cite our membership in the Association as evidence of professional competence, since the Association does not so certify any persons or organizations.
(2) We recognize our responsibility to contribute to the science of public opinion research and to disseminate as freely as possible the ideas and findings which emerge from our research.

D. The Respondent:

(1) We shall not lie to survey respondents or use practices and methods which abuse, coerce, or humiliate them.
(2) We shall protect the anonymity of every respondent, unless the respondent waives such anonymity for specified uses. In addition, we shall hold as privileged and confidential all information which tends to identify the respondent.

REFERENCES

American Statistical Association Conference on Human Population (1974) "Report on the ASA Conference on Surveys of Human Populations." *The American Statistician* 28: 30-34.

American Telephone and Telegraph (1980) *Notes on the Network.* Network Planning Division.

Aronson, Sidney (1977) "Bell's electrical toy: what's the use? The sociology of early telephone usage," pp. 15-39 in Ithiel de Sola Pool (ed.) *The Social Impact of the Telephone.* Cambridge, MA: MIT Press.

――― (1971) "The sociology of the telephone." *International Journal of Comparative Sociology* 12: 153-167.

Babbie, Earl R. (1979) *The Practice of Social Research.* Belmont, CA: Wadsworth.

――― (1973) *Survey Research Methods.* Belmont, CA: Wadsworth.

Backstrom, Charles H. and Gerald Hursh-Cesar (1981) *Survey Research* (2nd ed.). New York: John Wiley.

Bailer, Barbara, Leroy Bailey, and Joyce Stevens (1977) "Measures of interviewer bias and variance." *Journal of Marketing Research* 14: 337-343.

Ball, Donald W. (1968) "Toward a sociology of telephones and telephoners," pp. 59-75 in Marcello Truzzi (ed.) *Sociology and Everyday Life.* Englewood Cliffs, NJ: Prentice-Hall.

Becker, Theodore M. and Peter R. Meyers (1974) "Empathy and bravado: interviewing reluctant bureaucrats." *Public Opinion Quarterly* 38: 605-613.

Bell and Howell, Inc. (1981) *Phonofiche: Current Telephone Directories on Microfiche* Wooster, OH: Micro Photo Division.

Beza, Angel (1981) "Study design and telephone surveys." Presented at the Field Directors Conference, Santa Monica, CA (June).

Biel, Alexander L. (1969) "Abuses of survey research techniques: the phony interview." *Public Opinion Quarterly* 31: 298.

Blair, Ed (1979) "Testing interviewer effects in survey data." Presented at the annual meetings of the American Association for Public Opinion Research, Buck Hill Falls, PA (May).

Blankenship, Albert B. (1977) *Professional Telephone Surveys.* New York: McGraw-Hill.

――― (1976) "Listed vs. unlisted numbers in telephone survey samples." *Journal of Advertising Research* 17: 39-42.

――― and Michael M. Pearson (1977) "Guidelines for telephone group interviews." *Journal of the Academy of Marketing Science* 5: 1-8.

195

Bradburn, Norman M. (1977) "Respondent burden." *Health Survey Research Methods.* DHEW publication No. PSH 79-3207, pp. 57-61.

――― and William M. Mason (1964) "The effect of question-order on responses." *Journal of Marketing Research* 1: 57-61.

――― and Seymour Sudman (1979) *Improving Interview Method and Questionnaire Design.* San Francisco: Jossey-Bass.

Briggs, Asa (1977) "The pleasure telephone: a chapter in the prehistory of the media," pp. 40-65 in Ithiel de Sola Pool (ed.) *The Social Impact of the Telephone.* Cambridge, MA: MIT Press.

Brunner, James A. and G. Allen Brunner (1971) "Are voluntary unlisted telephone subscribers really different?" *Journal of Marketing Research* 8: 121-124.

――― and Stephen J. Carroll (1967) "The effect of prior telephone appointments on completion rates and response content." *Public Opinion Quarterly* 31: 562-564.

Bryant, Barbara E. (1975) "Respondent selection in a time of changing household composition." *Journal of Marketing Research* 12: 129-135.

Buffington, Larry G. (1980) "Sociology as expert knowledge: a case study." Presented at the meetings of the Pacific Sociological Association, San Francisco (April).

Campbell, Bruce A. (1981) "Race-of-interviewer effects among southern adolescents." *Public Opinion Quarterly* 45: 231-244.

Cannito, J. A. and K. L. Becker (1979) "The case for limited use of polls in the jury selection process." *Rutgers Journal of Computers, Technology and the Law* 7: 111-134.

Carroll, James D. (1973) "Confidentiality on social science research, sources and data: the Popkin case." *Political Science* 6: 268-280.

Colombotos, John (1969) "Personal versus telephone interviews: effect on responses." *Public Health Reports* 84: 773-782.

Coombs, Lolagene and Ronald Freedman (1964) "Use of telephone interviews in a longitudinal fertility study." *Public Opinion Quarterly* 28: 112-117.

Cooper, Sanford L. (1964) "Random sampling by telephone—an improved method." *Journal of Marketing Research* 1: 45-48.

DeJong, William (1979) "An examination of self-perception mediation of the foot-in-the-door effect." *Journal of Personality and Social Psychology* 37: 2221-2239.

DeMaio, Theresa J. (1980) "Refusals: who, where, and why." *Public Opinion Quarterly* 44: 223-233.

Deming, W. Edwards (1944) "On errors in surveys." *American Sociological Review* 9: 359-369.

Denitch, Bogdan (1972) "Elite interviewing and social structure: an example from Yugoslavia." *Public Opinion Quarterly* 36: 143-158.

Dexter, Lewis Anthony (1970) *Elite and Specialized Interviewing.* Evanston, IL: Northwestern University Press.

Dickson, John P., Michael Casey, Daniel Wyckoff, and William Wynd (1977) *Public Opinion Quarterly* 41: 100-106.

Dillman, Don A. (1981) "Mail surveys." Presented at the annual Field Directors' Conference. Santa Monica, CA (June).

――― (1978) *Mail and Telephone Surveys: The Total Design Method.* New York: John Wiley.

――― and James H. Frey (1974) "Coming of age: interviews by telephone." Presented at the annual meetings of the Pacific Sociological Association, San Jose, CA (March).

――― Jean Gallegos and James H. Frey (1976) "Reducing refusal rates for telephone interviews." *Public Opinion Quarterly* 40: 66-78.

Donald, Marjorie N. (1960) "Implications of nonresponse for the interpretation of mail questionnaire data." *Public Opinion Quarterly* 24: 99-114.

Dutka, Solomon (1980) "Business calls opinion surveys to testify for the defense." *Harvard Business Review* 58: 40-42.

Eastlack, J. O. and Henry Assael (1966) "Better telephone surveys through centralized interviewing." *Journal of Advertising Research* 6: 2-7.

Edwards, A. L. (1957) *The Social Desirability Variable in Personality Assessment and Research.* New York: Dryden.

Elshtain, Jean B. (1982) "Democracy and the QUBE tube." *Nation* 235: 108-110.

Fielder, Eve P. (1979) "Computer-assisted telephone interviewing: some implications for policy research." *PAIS*, no vol.: 662-668.

Fink, James C. (1981) "Quality improvement and time savings attributed to CATI―reflections on 11 years of experience." Presented at the 36th Annual Meetings of the American Association of Public Opinion Research, Buck Hill Falls, PA (May).

Frankel, Martin R. and Lester R. Frankel (1977) "Some recent developments in sample survey design." *Journal of Marketing Research* 14: 280-293.

Frey, James H. (1979) "Characteristics of listed versus unlisted households in a rapidly growing population." Presented at the annual meetings of the Pacific Sociological Association, Anaheim, CA (April).

Fuller, Carol H. (1974) "Effect of anonymity on return rate and response bias in a mail survey." *Journal of Applied Psychology* 59: 292-296.

Gallup, George (1947) "The quintamensional plan of question design." *Public Opinion Quarterly* II: 385-393.

Glasser, Gerald J. and Gale D. Metzger (1975) "National estimates of nonlisted telephone households and their characteristics." *Journal of Marketing Research* 12: 359-361.

Goldberg, David, Harry Sharp, and Ronald Freedman (1959) "The stability and reliability of expected family size data." *Milbank Memorial Fund Quarterly* 37: 369-385.

Gollin, Albert E. (1982) "Polling in the 1980's: straws in the wind." *AAPOR News* 9: 4-5.

――― (1980) "Exploring the liaison between polling and the press." *Public Opinion Quarterly* 44: 445-461.

Gorden, Raymond, L. (1980) *Interviewing: Strategy and Tactics* (3rd ed.). Homewood, IL: Dorsey.

Groves, Robert M. (1979) "Actors and questions in telephone and personal interview surveys." *Public Opinion Quarterly* 43: 190-205.

――― and Robert L. Kahn (1979) *Surveys By Telephone: A National Comparison With Personal Interviews.* New York: Academic Press.

Groves, Robert M. and Lou J. MagiLavy (1981) "Increasing response rates to telephone surveys: a door in the face for foot-in-the-door." *Public Opinion Quarterly* 45: 346-358.

Hagen, Dan E. and Charlotte M. Collier (1982) "Respondent selection procedures for telephone surveys: must they be intrusive?" Presented at the conference of the American Association for Public Opinion Research, Baltimore, MD (May).

Hatchett, Shirley and Howard Schuman (1975/76) "White respondents and race-of-interviewer effects." *Public Opinion Quarterly* 39: 523-528.

Hauck, Matthew and Michael Cox (1974) "Locating a sample by random digit dialing." *Public Opinion Quarterly* 38: 253-260.

Heberlein, Thomas A. and Robert Baumgartner (1978) "Factors affecting response rates to mailed questionnaires: a quantitative analysis of the published literature." *American Sociological Review* 43: 447-462.

Hiltz, Starr R. and Murry Turoff (1978) *The Network Nation: Human Communication Via Computer.* Reading, MA: Addison-Wesley.

Hochstim, Joseph R. (1967) "A critical comparison of three strategies of collecting data from households." *Journal of the American Statistical Association* 62: 976-989.

——— (1962) "Comparison of three information-gathering strategies in a population study of sociomedical variables." *Proceedings of the Social Statistics Section, American Statistical Association,* pp. 154-159.

Jolson, Marvin A. (1977) "How to double or triple mail-survey response rates." *Journal of Marketing* 41: 78-81.

Jordan, Lawrence A., Alfred C. Marcus, and Leo G. Reeder (1980) "Response styles in telephone and household interviewing: a field experiment." *Public Opinion Quarterly* 44: 210-222.

Kahn, Robert L. and Charles F. Cannell (1957) *The Dynamics of Interviewing.* New York: John Wiley.

Kalton, Graham, Martin Collins, and Lindsay Brook (1978) "Experiments in wording opinion questions." *Applied Statistics* 27: 149-161.

Katz, Daniel and Hadley Cantril (1937) "Public opinion polls." *Sociometry* 1: 155-179.

Kegeles, S. Stephen, Clinton F. Fink, and John P. Kirscht (1969) "Interviewing a national sample by long-distance telephone." *Public Opinion Quarterly* 33: 412-419.

Keller, Suzanne (1977) "The telephone in new (and old) communities," pp. 281-298 in Ithiel de Sola Pool (ed.) *The Social Impact of the Telephone.* Cambridge, MA: MIT Press.

Kerlinger, Fred N. (1965) *Foundations of Behavioral Research.* New York: Holt, Rinehart & Winston.

King, Francis W. (1970) "Anonymous versus identifiable questionnaires in drug usage surveys." *American Psychologist* 25: 982-985.

Kish, Leslie (1965) *Survey Sampling.* New York: John Wiley.

——— (1949) "A procedure for objective respondent selection within the household." *Journal of the American Statistical Association* 44: 380-387.

Klecka, William R. (1981) "Structured design considerations for questionnaires used in a computer-assisted survey environment." Presented at the annual field directors' conference, Santa Monica, CA (June).

——— and Alfred J. Tuchfarber, Jr. (1978) "Random digit dialing: A comparison to personal surveys." *Public Opinion Quarterly* 42: 105-114.

Kviz, F. J. (1977) "Toward a standard definition of response rate." *Public Opinion Quarterly* 41: 265-267.

Labaw, Patricia (1980) *Advanced Questionnaire Design*. Cambridge, MA: Abt.

Landon, E. Laird and Sharon K. Banks (1977) "Relative efficiency and bias of plus-one telephone sampling." *Journal of Marketing Research* 14: 294-299.

Leuthold, David A. and Raymond T. Scheele (1971) "Patterns of bias in samples based on telephone directories." *Public Opinion Quarterly* 35: 249-257.

Lucas, W. A. and W. C. Adams (1977) *An Assessment of Telephone Survey Methods*. Santa Monica, CA: Rand Corporation.

McFarland, Sam G. (1981) "Effects of question order on survey responses." *Public Opinion Quarterly* 45: 208-215.

McLuhan, Marshall (1964) *Understanding Media: The Extensions of Man*. London: Routledge & Kegan Paul.

Meyer, Martin (1977) "The telephone and the uses of time," pp. 225-245 in Ithiel de Sola Pool (ed.) *The Social Impact of the Telephone*. Cambridge, MA: MIT Press.

Nachmias, David and Chava Nachmias (1981) *Research Methods in the Social Sciences* (2nd ed.). New York: St. Martin's Press.

National Research Council (1979) *Privacy and Confidentiality as Factors in Survey Response*. Washington, DC: National Academy of Sciences.

Nejelski, Paul A. (1976) *Social Research in Conflict with Law and Ethics*. Cambridge, MA: Ballinger.

O'Neil, Michael J. (1979) "Varieties in random digit dialing sampling designs." Presented at the annual meetings of the American Association of Public Opinion Research, Buck Hill Falls, PA (May).

Parten, Mildred (1950) *Surveys, Polls and Samples*. New York: Harper & Row.

Payne, Stanley L. (1964) "Combination of survey methods." *Journal of Marketing Research* 1: 61-62.

——— (1951) *The Art of Asking Questions*. Princeton, NJ: Princeton University Press.

Perreault, William D., Jr. (1975) "Controlling order-effect bias." *Public Opinion Quarterly* 39: 544-551.

Perry, Charles R. (1977) "The British experience, 1876-1912: the impact of the telephone during the years of delay," pp. 69-96 in Ithiel de Sola Pool (ed.) *The Social Impact of the Telephone*. Cambridge, MA: MIT Press.

Phillips, Derek L. (1971) *Knowledge From What?* Chicago: Rand McNally.

Pound, Arthur (1926) *The Telephone Idea: Fifty Years Later*. New York: Greenberg.

Reamer, Frederick J. (1979) "Protecting research subjects and unintended consequences: the effect of guarantees of confidentiality." *Public Opinion Quarterly* 43: 497-506.

Reid, Seerley (1942) "Respondents and non-respondents to mail questionnaires." *Educational Research Bulletin* 21: 87-96.

Reingen, Peter H. and Jerome B. Kernan (1977) "Compliance with an interview request: a foot-in-the-door self perception interpretation." *Journal of Marketing Research* 14: 365-369.

Reynolds, Paul D. (1979) *Ethical Dilemmas and Social Science Research*. San Francisco: Jossey-Bass.

Rich, Clyde L. (1977) "Is random digit dialing really necessary?" *Journal of Marketing Research* 14: 300-305.

Rogers, Theresa F. (1976) "Interviews by telephone and in person: quality of responses and field performance." *Public Opinion Quarterly* 40: 51-65.

Rosenthal, Robert (1966) *Experimenter Effects in Behavior Research.* New York: Appleton-Century-Crofts.

Roslow, Sydney and Lawrence Roslow (1972) "Unlisted phone subscribers are different." *Journal of Advertising Research* 12: 35-38.

Schuman, Howard and Stanley Presser (1981) *Questions and Answers in Attitude Surveys: Experiments on Question Form, Wording and Context.* New York: Academic Press.

Sellitz, Claire, Lawrence S. Wrightsman, and Stuart W. Cook (1976) *Research Methods in Social Relations.* New York: Holt, Rinehart & Winston.

Sellitz, Claire, Marie Jahoda, Morton Deutsch, and Stuart W. Cook (1959) *Research Methods in Social Relations.* New York: Henry Holt.

Sewell, William H. and Vimal P. Shah (1968) "Socioeconomic status, intelligence and the attainment of higher education." *Sociology of Education* 40: 1-23.

Shanks, J. Merrill (1981) "The current status of computer-assisted telephone interviewing: recent progress, future prospects." Presented at the annual meetings of the American Association of Public Opinion Research, Buck Hill Falls, PA (May).

––– William L. Nichols, and Howard E. Freeman (1981) "The California disability survey: design and execution of a computer-assisted telephone survey." *Sociological Methods and Research* 10: 123-140.

Sharp, Laure M. and Joanne Frankel (1981) "Correlates of self-perceived respondent burden: findings from an empirical study." Presented at the annual meetings of the American Statistical Association, Detroit (August).

Shure, Gerald H. and Robert J. Meeker (1978) "A minicomputer system for multi-person computer-assisted telephone interviewing." *Behavior Research Methods and Instrumentation* 10: 196-202.

Siemiatycki, J. (1979) "A comparison of mail, telephone and home interview strategies for household health surveys." *American Journal of Public Health* 69: 238-245.

Sigelman, Lee (1981) "Question-order effects on presidential popularity." *Public Opinion Quarterly* 45: 199-207.

Simon, Julian L. (1978) *Basic Research Methods in Social Science* (2nd ed.). New York: Random House.

Singer, Eleanor and Luane Kohnke-Aquirre (1979) "Interviewer expectation effects: a replication and extension." *Public Opinion Quarterly* 43: 245-260.

Slocum, Walter L., L. T. Empey, and H. S. Swanson (1956) "Increasing response to questionnaires and structured interviews." *American Sociological Review* 21: 221-225.

Smead, Raymond J. and James Wilcox (1980) "Ring policy in telephone surveys." *Public Opinion Quarterly* 44: 115-116.

Sobal, Jeff (1978) "What should we say after we say hello? Disclosing information in interview introductions." Presented at the annual meetings of the American Association of Public Opinion Research, Buck Hill Falls, PA (June).

Sosdian, Carol P. and Laure M. Sharp (1980) "Nonresponse to mail surveys: access failure or respondent resistance?" *Public Opinion Quarterly* 44: 396-402.

Stafford, James E. (1966) "Influence of preliminary contact on mail returns." *Journal of Marketing Research* 3: 410-411.

Steeh, C. G. (1981) "Trends in nonresponse rates: 1952-1979." *Public Opinion Quarterly* 45: 40-57.

Suchman, Edward A. and Boyd McCandless (1940) "Who answers questionnaires?" *Journal of Applied Psychology* 24: 758-769.

Sudman, Seymour (1976) *Applied Sampling.* New York: Academic Press.

——— (1966) "New uses of telephone methods in survey research." *Journal of Marketing Research* 3: 163-167.

——— and Norman M. Bradburn (1974) *Response Effects in Surveys.* Chicago: Aldine.

Sudman, Seymour, Norman M. Bradburn, Ed Blair, and Carol Stocking (1977) "Modest expectations: the effects of interviewers' prior expectations on response." *Sociological Methods and Research* 6: 177-182.

Survey Research Laboratory (1981) "Current research." *Survey Research* 13: 15.

Tremblay, Kenneth R. and Don A. Dillman (1977) "Research ethics: emerging concerns from increased use of mail and telephone survey methods." *Humboldt Journal of Social Relations* 5: 65-84.

Troldahl, Verling C. and Roy C. Carter (1964) "Random selection of respondents within households in phone surveys." *Journal of Marketing Research* 1: 71-76.

Tull, Donald S. and Gerald S. Albaum (1977) "Bias in random digit dialed surveys." *Public Opinion Quarterly* 41: 389-395.

United Nations (1981) *Statistical Yearbook* (31st ed.). New York.

U.S. Bureau of the Census (1981) *Statistical Abstract of the United States—1980* (101st ed.). Washington, DC: Department of Commerce.

U.S. Department of Health, Education and Welfare (DHEW) (1971) *The Institutional Guide to D.H.E.W. Policy on Protection of Human Subjects.* Washington, DC: National Institutes of Health.

Vigderhous, Gideon (1981) "Scheduling phone interviews: a study of seasonal patterns." *Public Opinion Quarterly* 45: 250-259.

Waisanen, F. B. (1954) "A note on the response to a mailed questionnaire." *Public Opinion Quarterly* 18: 210-212.

Waksberg, Joseph (1978) "Sampling methods for random digit dialing." *Journal of the American Statistical Association* 73: 40-46.

Weeks, Michael F. and R. Paul Moore (1981) "Ethnicity-of-interviewer effects on ethnic respondents." *Public Opinion Quarterly* 45: 245-249.

Weeks, Michael F., B. L. Jones, R. E. Folson, Jr., and C. H. Benrud (1980) "Optimal times to contact sample households." *Public Opinion Quarterly* 44: 101-114.

Wildman, Richard C. (1977) "Effects of anonymity and social setting on survey responses." *Public Opinion Quarterly* 41: 74-79.

Wiseman, Frederick (1972) "Methodological bias in public opinion surveys." *Public Opinion Quarterly* 34: 105-108.

——— and Phillip McDonald (1979) "Noncontact and refusal rates in consumer telephone surveys." *Journal of Marketing Research* 16: 478-484.

Zuckerman, Harriet (1972) "Interviewing an ultra-elite." *Public Opinion Quarterly* 36: 159-175.

AUTHOR INDEX

Adams, W. C. 51, 141
Albaum, Gerald S. 36
American Statistical Association 24
American Telephone and Telegraph 59
Aronson, Sidney 10, 11, 12, 13
Assael, Henry 140

Babbie, Earl R. 18, 64, 88, 116, 149
Backstrom, Charles H. 18, 88, 149
Bailar, Barbara 47, 149
Ball, Donald W. 16, 17
Banks, Sharon K. 67
Baumgartner, Robert 40, 48
Becker, K. L. 183
Becker, Theodore, M. 43
Bell and Howell, Inc. 59
Beza, Angel 23
Biel, Alexander L. 174
Blair, Ed 149
Blankenship, Albert B. 62, 66, 139, 143,
    171, 182, 186
Bradburn, Norman M. 88, 109, 110,
    111, 127, 185
Briggs, Asa 10, 11
Brunner, G. Allen 21, 62
Brunner, James A. 62
Bryant, Barbara E. 80
Buffington, Larry G. 184

Campbell, Bruce A. 46
Cannell, Charles F. 112
Cannito, J. A. 183
Cantril, Hadley 19
Carroll, James D. 181
Carroll, Steven J. 21
Carter, Roy E. 80, 83
Collier, Charlotte M. 83

Colombotos, John 48
Coombs, Lolagene 22
Cooper, Sanford L. 60, 71, 72, 76
Cox, Michael 25, 73, 76

DeJong, William 127
DeMaio, Theresa J. 41
Deming, W. Edwards 127
Denitch, Bogdan 43
Dexter, Lewis Anthony 43
Dickson, John P. 188
Dillman, Don A. 18, 21, 23, 28, 31, 34,
    39, 40, 48, 60, 64, 66, 90, 91, 92,
    93, 101, 105, 116, 119, 120, 123,
    124, 141, 149, 150, 178, 185, 186
Donald, Marjorie N. 20
Dutka, Solomon 183, 184

Eastlack, J. O. 140
Edwards, A. L. 50
Elshtain, Jean G. 176

Fielder, Eve P. 145, 146, 148, 169
Fink, James C. 144
Frankel, Joanne 185
Frankel, Lester R. 58, 74
Frankel, Martin R. 58, 74
Freedman, Ronald 22
Frey, James H. 21, 62
Fuller, Carol H. 50

Gallup, George 111
Glasser, Gerald J. 62
Goldberg, David 22
Gollin, Albert E. 177
Gorden, Raymond L. 149

Groves, Robert M. 23, 24, 27, 31, 36, 39, 41, 44, 46, 47, 51, 52, 53, 55, 62, 68, 76, 83, 91, 94, 95, 123, 185

Hagen, Dan E. 83
Hatchett, Shirley 46
Hauck, Matthew 25, 73, 76
Heberlein, Thomas A. 40, 48
Hiltz, Starr R. 176, 186
Hochstim, Joseph R. 27, 31, 51
Hursh-Cesar, Gerald 18, 88, 149

Jolson, Marvin A. 21
Jordan, Lawrence A. 47, 48, 51

Kahn, Robert L. 23, 24, 27, 31, 36, 39, 41, 44, 46, 47, 51, 52, 53, 55, 62, 68, 76, 83, 91, 112, 185
Kalton, Graham 111, 112
Katz, Daniel 19
Kegeles, S. Stephen 18, 22
Keller, Suzanne 14
Kerlinger, Fred N. 18
Kernan, Jerome B. 94
King, Francis W. 50
Kish, Leslie 78
Klecka, William R. 31, 148
Kohnke-Aquirre, Luane 47
Kz, F. J. 38

Labaw, Patricia J. 89, 90 Landon, E.
LairdLandon, E. Laird 67
Leuthold, David A. 61
Lucas, W. A. 51, 141

MagiLavy, Lou J. 94, 95
Mason, William 110, 111
Meyer, Martin 14
McCandless, Boyd 20
McDonald, Phillip 41, 42, 164
McFarland, Sam G. 112
McLuhan, Marshall 10, 14, 15, 16
Meeker, Robert J. 144, 169
Metzger, Gald D. 62
Meyers, Peter R. 43
Moore, R. Paul 46

Nachmias, Chava 179

Nachmias, David 179
National Research Council 71, 181, 182
Nejelski, Paul A. 182

O'Neil, Michael J. 69, 73, 74, 76

Parten, Mildred 18, 98
Payne, Stanley L. 22, 88, 116
Pearson, Michael M. 186
Perreault, William D., Jr. 109, 110
Perry, Charles R. 13
Phillips, Derek L. 127
Pound, Arthur 13
Presser, Stanley 102, 103, 109, 110, 111, 116, 121, 127

Reamer, Frederick J. 181
Reid, Seerley 20
Reingen, Peter H. 94
Reynolds, Paul D. 177
Rich, Clyde L. 62
Rogers, Theresa F. 46, 47, 48, 52
Rosenthal, Robert 127
Roslow, Laurence 62
Roslow, Sydney 62

Scheele, Raymond T. 61
Schuman, Howard 46, 102, 103, 109, 110, 111, 116, 121, 123
Sellitz, Claire 18
Sewell, William H. 22
Shah, Vimal P. 22
Shanks, J. Merrill 144, 147, 148, 169
Sharp, Laure M. 26, 38, 185
Shure, Gerald H. 144
Siemiatycki, J. 20, 27, 31, 39, 47, 51
Sigelman, Lee 109, 110
Simon, Julian 19, 48, 49, 53
Singer, Eleanor 47
Slocum, Walter L. 21, 22
Smead, Raymond J. 161
Sobal, Jeff 98
Sosdian, Carol P. 26, 38
Stafford James E. 21
Steeh, C. G. 41
Suchman, Edward A. 20

Sudman, Seymour 20, 21, 47, 58, 60, 61, 73, 88, 109, 127
Survey Research Laboratory 169

Tremblay, Kenneth R. 178
Troldahl, Verling C. 80, 83
Tuchfarber, Alfred J. 31
Tull, Donald S. 36
Turoff, Murray 176, 186

United Nations 13
United States Bureau of the Census 13, 22, 36

United States Department of Health Education and Welfare (DHEW) 178, 179
Vigderhous, Gideon 164

Waisanen, F. B. 21
Waksberg, Joseph 74, 75
Weeks, Michael F. 46, 164
Wilcox, James 161
Wildman, Richard C. 50
Wiseman, Frederick 41, 42, 46, 51, 164

Zuckerman, Harriet 43

SUBJECT INDEX

Amrigon, Inc. 144
American Telephone and Telegraph 12, 59, 85
Audits and Surveys, Inc. 144

Berkeley Survey Research Center 144

California disability study 148
Centralized interviewing facility 45, 47, 139
Chilton, Inc. 143, 144
Code of ethics 177-178
Coding 166-167
Common Channel Interoffice Signaling (CCIS) 175
Completion rates
    calculation of 38
    comparison of mail, telephone and face-to-face surveys 38-39, 54
Computer Assisted Survey Methods (CSM) 144
Computer Assisted Telephone Interviewing (CATI) 24, 25, 34, 52, 129, 139, 143-149, 172, 177, 184
Computerized conferencing 176
Computerized dialing 173
Confidentiality 148, 180-185
    as expressed in introduction to questionnaire 94, 98
    comparison of mail, telephone and face-to-face surveys 49-50, 54

Data analysis 166-168
    Statistical Package for Social Sciences (SPSS) 166

Data quality
    comparison of mail, telephone and face-to-face surveys 44-53, 54
Directory of Directories 59

Informed consent 97, 178-180
"Instant" polls 177
Instructions to interviewers: 153-161
    on questionnaires 100
Interviewer error 89
Interviewing 149-166
    calling record 159
    computerization 148, 172-173
    group 176, 186
    guidelines 154-159
    scheduling 161-166
Interviewers:
    characteristics 150-151
    pool of 150, 152
    recruiting 149-152
    supervision 44-45, 143
    training 153-161
Introduction to questionnaire: 91-100
    amount of information 98-100
    "foot-in-the-door" technique 95
    no pre-interview contact 95-98
    pre-interview contact 92-95
Invasion of privacy 177
Item nonresponse
    comparison of mail, telephone and face-to-face survey 46-48, 54

"Junk" phone calls 18-19, 22

Literary Digest 18-19, 22
Long Line Directory 68, 69, 75

Marc, Inc. 144

Network Guide 68
Noncontact rates
  calcultation of 42
  comparison of mail, telephone and
    face-to-face surveys 42-43, 54

Phony interview 174, 178, 186
Pretesting 126
Probing 51, 53

Quality control 44-45, 139-149
QUBE 176
Question order 100-116
  first questions 103-106
  general-specific sequence 110-113
  grouping of 106-108
  guidelines 115
Question order effect 109
  consistency 110
  contrast 112
  definition 109
  fatigue 110
  redundancy 111
  saliency 111
Questions: 116-127
  basis for inclusion in questionnaire
    118-119
  closed-end 105
  complex 52, 112-114, 119-125
  demographic 114
  key word summary for complex
    questions 120-121
  open-end 105
  sensitive 51, 113-114
  split questions 123-124
  wording problems 125-127
Questionnaire design
  coders' needs 90, 100-102
  guidelines 115
  interviewers' needs 88-89, 100
  introductions 88, 91-100
  respondents' needs 88-89, 100-102
  use of transitional statements
    106-108
Questionnaire length
  comparison of mail, telephone and

face-to-face surveys 48-49, 54, 136

Random Digit Dialing (RDD) 23, 68-76, 129
  comparison of designs 77
  simple random sample design 69-71
  Sudman method 73-74
  Waksberg design 74-76
  with Cross Reference Directory 71-73
Refusal rates
  comparison of mail, telephone and
    face-to-face surveys 40-41, 54
Respondent burden 119-125
Response order 121-125
  hypothetical scale 123-124
  recency or primary effect 121
  response effects 121
  split question 123
  unfolding technique 123
Response rates
  calculation of 38
  comparison of mail, telephone and
    face-to-face surveys 38-40, 54
Robotics 176

Sample size 135, 136
Sampling 57-85
  comparison of mail, telephone and
    face-to-face surveys 35-44, 54
  design effects (DEFTS) 76
  nonprobability 58
Sampling error 39, 76, 84
Sampling from lists 58-68
  add-a-digit sampling 67-68
  problems of lists 58-62
  simple random sample 63-64
  systematic sample 64-67
Sampling within households 43-44, 78-84
Social desirability of response
  comparison of mail, telephone and
    face-to-face surveys 45-46, 54
Survey costs
  comparison of mail, face-to-face and
    telephone surveys 28-30, 54

Survey implementation time
  comparison of mail, telephone and face-to-face surveys 33-34, 54
Survey personnel requirements
  comparison of mail, telephone and face-to-face surveys 31-33, 54
Surveys, face-to-face
  comparison of mail and telephone surveys 27-55
  lowered acceptance of 23-24
  past use of 20
Surveys in court 180-185
  survey researcher as expert witness 184
Surveys, mail
  comparison to face-to-face and telephone surveys 27-55
Surveys, telephone
  activity checklist 131
  administration 129-169
  administrative plan 130-139
  budget 131-138
  comparison to mail and face-to-face surveys 27-55
  ethical issues 177-185
  increased use of 18-25
  needed research 185-185

project cost estimates 138
quality control 139-149

Telephone
  behavior related to 14-17
  distribution of 13, 22-23, 36
  history 9-13
  impact on social relations 13-15
  norms guiding usage 15-17
  previous use in research 20-22
  technological developments 172-177
"Total design method" (TDM) 23, 39

University of California, Berkeley 144, 148
University of California, Los Angeles 144, 148
University of Michigan 23, 39, 144
University of Nevada Telephone Survey Center 99, 131, 137, 152, 155
University of Wisconsin 144, 169

Videophone 175-176

Wide Area Telephone Service (WATS) 24, 139, 142-143, 169

ABOUT THE AUTHOR

James H. Frey is an Associate Professor of Sociology and Director of the Telephone Survey Center at the University of Nevada, Las Vegas. He is the author of *An Organizational Analysis of University-Environment Relations* (1977), *The Governance of Intercollegiate Athletics* (1982), and articles on survey research, deviance, and sport sociology. His current research interests are in the areas of organizational deviance, higher education, and the social determinants of gambling behavior.